The
William Edward Reis
Library

Allegheny College

DENMARK

Kingdom of Reason

WITHDRAWN

914.89
R744d

DENMARK

Kingdom of Reason

BY AGNES ROTHERY

THE VIKING PRESS · NEW YORK

1937

THE PHOTOGRAPHS IN THIS BOOK ARE BY HARRY ROGERS PRATT

FIRST PUBLISHED APRIL 1937

COPYRIGHT 1937 BY AGNES ROTHERY PRATT

PRINTED IN THE UNITED STATES OF AMERICA

DISTRIBUTED IN CANADA BY THE MACMILLAN COMPANY

OF CANADA, LTD.

TO

CHR. H. OLESEN

59002

CONTENTS

ILLUSTRATIONS

ix

A LITTLE CANDLE THROWS ITS
BEAMS

DENMARK, the oldest kingdom in the world, is also one of the wisest and happiest.

In a universe pitching in unrest she maintains her equilibrium. In a Europe seething with hatred and riven by distress she blooms in contentment and cheerful industry.

For years travellers have delighted in this prettiest of countrysides, out of which grow brown-thatched or red-tiled farmhouses as cosily as berries on a branch. For years students of social legislation, agricultural co-operation, and the adult high school have been studying a land which, unendowed by natural riches, is increasingly and steadily productive with a population—a mere speck among the hungry hordes of the globe—not only clothed and fed but smiling.

Now everyone is suddenly curious about such a phenomenon. Commissions are rushing over by the boatload to investigate how Denmark does it, and holiday-seekers, wearied by the lamentations and confusion of their own countries, are hastening to enjoy an interim of rational and merry living. Denmark is too homogeneous and too small to be a model for countries of vaster proportions and more variegated problems, but she can serve as a candle, shining like a good deed in a world far naughtier than it should be.

PART I

The Golden Crown

CHAPTER ONE

COPENHAGEN

COPPER-GREEN roofs and copper-green spires: towers pointed, squared, squat, slender: steeples twisted, rounded, garlanded with golden balls: domes, turrets, minarets—pierced, swelling, crenellated—all of copper-green, picked out with gold, crowned with gold, embellished with golden clocks and golden coronets!

Bishop Absalon, who founded Copenhagen eight hundred years ago, loved towers, and so have all the Copenhageners who have lived there ever since.

Sharply pitched shop roofs of weathered red tile: mansard palace roofs of weathered slate: windows formed of sculptured stone: skylights bright with plants within and window boxes without, and, in the very midst of the crowding roofs and steeples, crowds of masts with flags and pennants, with sails furled or flapping, marking the canals which bisect and intersect the traffic of the streets! Surprisingly, upon such old-world picturesqueness, there is stamped—in the shop windows, in the lettering on signs and advertisements, in the appearance of men and women on the streets—the undeniable dash and modernity of an up-to-date metropolis.

3

The Golden Crown

What more pleasing way to learn the sections and directions of that jumbled congeries of buildings which remain not from the first or the second capital, but from the seventeenth- and eighteenth-century Copenhagen, than by taking a spire for an objective and starting for it? The street—one of many radii from the central Kongens Nytorv—leads with deceptive simplicity between shop windows glittering with silver dishes and silver spoons, billowing with the prettily glazed blue-and-white porcelain we have called "Copenhagen" since childhood; hesitates at an open square with a fountain ringed by bronze storks and enclosed with buildings, some new, some old, but all substantial, well cared for and splashed with flowering balconies. Across the square, keeping the chosen street carefully in mind—does it swerve a bit?—passing a sidewalk café, where, under a striped awning, people are drinking coffee, past a shop window twinkling with intricately shaped and decorated Danish cakes, another strung with golden-brown herring, another with more silver dishes, another with more silver spoons—out into another square with another fountain. Around it, under an arcade—now the spire is momentarily lost—and our attention is caught by a golden boot hanging above a door—a shoemaker's symbol—while next to it a golden plate with a notch in the rim proclaims a barber shop. That swinging bunch of golden grapes is the sign of a vintner and the twisted golden "Kringle" yonder must be a bakery. But wait! Is this our street? It nods reassurance and trustingly we follow it, to emerge in a suddenly spacious plaza whose whole centre is a pageant of open stalls "with roses and lilies all ablowing." Slowly now—where is the spire? The street beckons. Here you are! Over an ancient balustraded bridge—who can resist pausing for a moment to watch the fishing-boats wedged tight as matches in a box along the canal? The street marches on—straight as a die—conducts itself anew past an ivied fence, indicates a tempting short cut and promises to meet you at the other end. Down the short cut—more swinging golden symbols, more windows with silver spoons, and you are in a great cobbled square with a statue instead of a fountain in the centre and there, plainly to be seen ahead, is your spire. Only, instead of being baroque, it is twisted like a corkscrew, and twisted in the wrong direction at that! And instead of a golden crown on top of it, it has a golden figure! Come, come! This is quite wrong. You turn around slowly, carefully. Ah, there is your spire! Only now it is neither baroque nor corkscrewed, but is nothing less than the tails of four mythological dragons, twisted together and rearing their coils against a sky as innocently blue and white as blue-and-white porcelain. This is absurd. You look for your street. It has darted off and disappeared around a corner and left you—where? You cannot see the woods for the trees. Now find your way back! Pick another spire for an objective. Remember the travellers lost in forests who tramp round and round in circles. Is that your street, playing hide-and-seek and laughing at you with staccato golden jeers? No, it is the clock in a distant invisible tower, striking the quarter hour. What quarter? What hour? A steeplechase indeed!

Copenhagen, however, is something more than copper-green roofs, enticing streets, sidewalk cafés, and flower markets! Its antiquity is honourable and its modernity admirable. It is not only the largest city in Denmark—more than a quarter, almost a third, of the entire population live in the capital—it is one of the busiest of merchant towns, one of the gayest of pleasure towns in all Europe. Its harbour is the largest in the Baltic. Into its Free Port come goods for transhipment to and from

every country, and up and down the Öresund, which lies between Denmark and Sweden, pass ships from all over the
world. After nearly nine hundred years, it is still worthy of the
name of Copenhagen, which means "Merchants' Harbour."

To know the history of Copenhagen, one must know the
history of Denmark. And what foreigner, in this day of haste,
will take the time to read—much less to master—a chronology
which begins two thousand years before the birth of Christ and
is solidly packed with events, personalities, acquisition of territory and loss of territory, and wars—repeated wars—with every
single country in Europe except France? But even to the ignorant, Copenhagen is delightful. While there is no other
foreign city where the English-speaking person feels so immediately at home, the same is true for a Swede or a Norwegian,
a German or a Hollander. Even the French, who love only
France, enjoy Copenhagen. For the great vivacious capital of
the small and sensible kingdom has the charm of a woman born
comely and growing in grace with the years, who expresses her
happiness by giving pleasure to all about her: to her family,
her children, her friends, even to the stranger who, unan-
nounced, rushes in and rushes out and for long, long after-
wards marvels at his friendly welcome.

This intimacy is not entirely derived from the city's accessibility and pleasing appearance. It is partly due to tempo,
and that tempo is created by a million rubber-tired whirling
wheels, a million flashing legs, a million pedalling feet. Like
the sands of the desert before the wind, the bicycles of Copenhagen scud down the streets. Yellow-haired girls, holding down
their fluttering skirts; "scorching" boys bent over their handlebars; delivery men pushing trucks before them or pulling
trailers behind them; business men with canes; chimney-

sweeps with brooms; clerks with briefcases; housewives with shopping baskets; a white-uniformed nurse racing the stork; a red-jacketed postman; a soldier in uniform; a woman with a baby strapped into a basket seat in front, perilously suggesting a bumper; another with a puppy in a similar position—on—on they come, singly, in groups, in files, in masses, darting in and out among the motor cars, buses and trams and pedestrians, with breath-taking insouciance. No good for taxi-drivers to blow their horns. They can't blow four hundred thousand bicycles off the streets of Copenhagen. No good for a chauffeur to fret and fume, for all cyclists are descendants of that King Canute who raised his hand to motion the tide to recede. But the gesture of King Canute, despite his sceptre and crown, was impotent, while in Copenhagen that of a workman in wooden shoes or a girl in high-heeled slippers, if only they are on bi-cycles, has power to stop the largest motor bus. From the time an infant is lifted to his basket seat on his mother's handlebars, all during the period he is learning on his own small wheel— his father's hand upon his shoulder—to negotiate the intri-cacies of traffic, up through speeding youth and portly middle age to octogenarianism, the bicyclist is specially privileged. Surely if a criminal were seeking sanctuary in Copenhagen, he need not fly to a cathedral. He need merely mount his wheel and hold up his hand, and doubtless the police car would, through sheer force of habit, pause or at least swerve to let him pass. In Copenhagen? All Denmark, with its level roads and specially marked paths, is alive with cycles, and while certain ladies of fifty lament that at their advanced age they can pedal for only four or five hours now without getting a little tired, not long ago a woman of seventy-five bicycled from Viborg in Jutland to Copenhagen, a distance of about one hundred and sixty-five miles, in two days, and dismounted none the worse for wear.

Although all the four hundred thousand bicycles seem to be in motion every hour, as a matter of fact their disposition when not in use constitutes one of the characteristic sights and problems of the city. Ranged in stands by the score outside office buildings and apartment houses, parked by hundreds in amusement parks, piled up in front of restaurants in a jumble as indistinguishable as Japanese shoes outside a temple, demanding space under cover in winter, they must be considered in all their arrangements by the city-planners and architects. But the stranger becomes so accustomed to them that soon he notices them no more than leaves fluttering on trees or ripples moving over the water. But at first his fancy toys with strange juxtapositions. Do judge and lawyer, juror and accused, all bowl to court? Do the teacher and his pupils pedal to school? And what about the King? Does he, with ermine robe flying, with his crown on his head, bicycle through the streets of Copenhagen? No, as a matter of fact the King rides on a horse, leaving his royal residence at eight o'clock in the morning and cantering through the street quite unassumingly and unaccompanied. The royal residence is not that vast Christiansborg Palace with its golden crown against the sky. Upon this spot Bishop Absalon built a fortress (in 1167), bits of which may still be seen in the basement of the present Christiansborg. When Christian VI raised his castle on this same spot (1733), it grew to such extent and elaboration that at last he refused to hear what it was costing and every Saturday burned the bills that had accumulated during the week. Although this was destroyed by fire sixty-one years later, the original Court of Honour, enclosed by two colonnaded wings extending to the

Marble Bridge, still exists to remind us of that costly splendour. The palace which replaced it was also burned (1884), and this present mighty edifice was completed only in 1928. Here sit both Houses of Parliament and the Supreme Court. The Ministry of Foreign Affairs has its office here, and in the royal reception-rooms the King twice a month holds his public audiences.

He lives, however, a short distance away in Amalienborg Palace, one of four large and lovely rococo buildings, all identical and surrounding a courtyard, which, although it is dignified by a pillared entrance spanning the avenue of Amaliegade, is in no way shut off from public use. The location of Amalienborg Palace, in neighbourly proximity not only to the various Legations but to quite everyday houses, hotels, and shops, and also to the busy water front, so that from certain angles it seems quite in the midst of masts and funnels and warehouses, is characteristic of the attitude of the people to the King and the King to the people. Not that Court life has been levelled down to the handshaking and business suits of a republic. The oldest kingdom in the world—a kingdom which has never known foreign domination—preserves with pride the panoply of its royal tradition. While economists from the confused countries of Europe and the Americas are trooping to Denmark to study its enlightened legislation, that clever little kingdom manages to enjoy the benefits of a social democracy without sacrificing the stability of a dynastic ruler or losing the colour and ceremonial of what Whitelaw Reid called "a delightful little Dresden china Court." The King is honoured during his lifetime and in death is given majestic entombment in Roskilde Cathedral. And he, on his part, fills his role as a sovereign with dignity, and exercises with discretion his carefully prescribed power as a ruler. The golden crown, not only as regal insignia but as a popular decoration, glitters everywhere, and in Copenhagen not only a cat may look at a Queen but almost anybody may look at a King by glancing out of the window at eight o'clock in the morning.

Nevertheless, it is not for its royal family so much as for its other inhabitants that Copenhagen spends most of its money and thoughtful care. What it does for them in the way of free schools, free hospitals, free homes for the aged, demands another chapter. What it does for their entertainment and in recognition of their right to pleasure is enjoyably apparent to the most casual visitor, since he, too, may, any fine day, stroll along the Langelinie, that promenade bright with flowering trees and shrubs and the uniforms of soldiers and sailors and gaily dressed girls, and overlooking a sea animated by sail boats, motor boats, steamers, freighters, tramps, private yachts, visiting training-ships, and friendly war ships, by racing-shells rowed by girls and canoes paddled by athletes dipping double-bladed oars, by four-masted schooners bringing wood from Finland, by ferries bringing visitors from Sweden and luxury liners bringing tourists from the other side of the world.

Overlooking this flutter of sails and flags and pennants, diplomats and débutantes stroll along the Langelinie, mingling with clerks and mothers pushing perambulators. It is a true European promenade, unmarred by rudeness or ostentation. Some of the strollers pause to buy a bottle of milk at a kiosk, drinking it through a straw, and others take coffee on the terrace of the Royal Yacht Club—all of them alike in not seeking to be amused but amusing themselves. One end of the Langelinie, near the English Church, is marked by a fountain representing Gefion, that legendary Asawoman who, receiving

permission to take as much of Sweden as she could plough
around in a single day, transformed her four sons into four
bulls and with them ploughed out the island of Zealand upon
which Copenhagen stands. The colossal statue shows her not
only driving her metamorphosed progeny through tremendous
spuming furrows, but cracking her whip above them with a
right goodwill. The other end of the promenade is marked
by a quite different feminine form, for here, on a natural
boulder by the water's edge, sits in wave-wetted bronze the
Little Mermaid who chose to sacrifice her finny tail for human feet so that she could follow her human lover even
though every step was to be torture and although

> *"She left lonely for ever*
> *The kings of the sea."*

The Danish girls who swing along the Langelinie are modelled more after Gefion than the Little Mermaid—with their
strong bodies and firm necks. Nature has crowned them with
hair shading from red-gold to yellow-gold to white-gold, and
the hairdresser has added a final burnishing so that the present
hatless fashion delights both the possessors and the observers
of these sunny heads. Neither are the men afraid of their special hirsute prerogative and many a well-kept beard imparts a
Viking nobility to its possessor.

The Langelinie is not unique in being crowded. The principal streets of Copenhagen are always thronged, for although
Denmark has only a little over three and a half million inhabitants the capital claims almost a million of them—all of them,
the distracted foreigner is inclined to think, named Hansen,
Nielsen, Jensen, or Rasmussen.

This sense of a crowded population is augmented by the

tens, scores, hundreds of replicas of the human form, fanciful, legendary, and historical. There never was such a city of statues! They are on pedestals in parks and plazas; they are hoisted on roofs; they recline, sit, ride horseback, exhort. Their figures are full length in bronze above pediments, and their faces are in relief in stone above doors and windows, and their busts are everywhere. They are in capes and copes and stovepipe hats. Above the Raadhus is a row of watchmen of the city with long-handled maces. In Saint Anne's Plads, Niels Gade holds his baton; in the King's Garden, Hans Christian Andersen holds a book. Here is a tangible immortality any Dane may believe in and apparently almost any Dane may achieve. In fact, one wonders uneasily if, in another century or two, there will not be more people up in the air than down in the street. But while the men of bronze and stone may be honoured by their elevation, they are deprived of one of the fundamental enjoyments of their more ephemeral brothers below. No longer can they sit in the sidewalk cafés that, with the flowers of spring, sprout up on every corner, balcony, and terrace, and tuck away a platterful of those open sandwiches so dear to the eye and palate of all Danes, especially when accompanied by a glass of beer or a thimbleful of *akvavit*. Possibly up aloft there they may catch the aroma of the best coffee on the continent of Europe, but that must be poor consolation. And all the staggering array of fish and crustaceans, of meat and fowl, of cheeses, wines, and cakes, which follow each other in caloric redundancy, are denied them. For the Danes pay great attention to food. They prepare it with thoughtfulness and a great deal of butter. They serve it with care and more butter. And they consume it with satisfaction and more butter. There are agreeable eating-places everywhere, not only for those residents

One of Copenhagen's many fountains. This one is ringed with bronze storks.

ALLEGHENY COLLEGE LIBRARY

Like the sands of the desert before the wind, the bicycles of
Copenhagen scud down the streets.

ALLEGHENY·COLLEGE LIBRARY

Frederiksborg Castle, one of the splendid structures of North Zealand.

ALLEGHENY COLLEGE LIBRARY

Behind the audience at the Peacock Theatre stands the beloved
Pierrot of Tivoli.

ALLEGHENY COLLEGE LIBRARY

or visitors who gravitate to the most fashionable hotels, but
for the family of modest means trooping into a restaurant for
Sunday night supper after a day in the beech woods; for the
little old spinster who, after finishing a frugal meal at home,
orders a dessert of a cup of coffee and a plate of strawberries
in the cheer of a café. There are even, in this meat-eating city,
vegetarian restaurants for clients of special digestions and
convictions—although it must be admitted that vegetables are
soaked and stewed out of all their succulence and flavour, in
the traditional English manner. Whether the Danes were
contaminated in this by their cousins across the Channel, or
vice versa, is a melancholy debate. But what they omit in this
branch of the culinary art, they make up for in the manner
of serving. The head waiter, august, vigilant, presides over
the ritual of the restaurant. His underlings skim and fly
through their ministrations, bearing mysterious vessels aloft—
novitiates striving ever upward and onward towards ultimate
ordination, while the congregation obeys the injunction to
"eat what you will and suffer what you must."

Over all these substantial people of bronze and stone and
flesh and blood, over all this massive architecture, under and
over and shot through the whole practical mundane fabric
of living, floats, paradoxically, a ribbon of illusion, iridescent
as gauze. For all Copenhagen is enveloped in the tissue of a
fairy-tale. This is not entirely because the shepherdesses and
chimney-sweeps, the emperor and the nightingale, the duckling
and the swan of Hans Christian Andersen may be seen in porcelain in the shop windows, in frescoes on café walls, and in
the names of cakes and candies. It is because the Danish taste
inclines to fanciful effects and the Danish heart to sage simplicity, so that glittering brass balustrades give a prosaic stair

the suggestion of a magic ascent, and twisted dragon tails seem quite a proper finish for a sober Bourse. The gilded grapes and boots and barbers' plates suspended over the sidewalks, the gilded wings and crowns, are like pictures in a child's story-book. Even the automats with geysers of beer and fruit juice, and appearing and disappearing shelves of strange viands, remind us of gingerbread houses through which one must munch a pathway before reaching the enchanted wood beyond. And what shall be said of the street fountain in whose waters, once a year on the King's birthday, dance golden balls for every child to see? And what shall be said of Rosenborg Castle, complete on the outside with turrets and roses and a moat, and complete on the inside with thrones and sceptre and swords? It is no good to tell us it was built by a mortal king in 1606. We are sure it rose from the garden at the wave of a wand, with its tower rooms and winding stairs and silver chairs and marble floors, with its rooms like jewel-boxes padded with ivories, porcelains, paintings, crystals, enamels, diamonds, and pearls. Here is Ali Baba's cave and Jack and the Beanstalk's kingdom. And here good boys and girls may see silver lions life-size; glass delicate as cobwebs hung with dewdrops; furniture carved, lacquered, inlaid, decorated with every conceivable elaboration; vases as tall as a man and lanterns twice as tall; brocades and velvets worn by kings, and crowns and armour worn by princes. It is no good to tell us that this is the Chronological Collection of the Danish Kings, or to add that craftsmen and artists find motifs and inspiration here. We know quite well that Rosenborg with its crystal cabinets and glittering gems and all its 9930 catalogued items is the castle of a fairy-tale, and although adults may be wearied by too much repetition—even the repetition of gold and silver

and jewels—few would be so churlish as to criticize this fulfilment of childhood's image of Faerie.

While all the substantial fabric of Copenhagen is shot
through with sparkling threads of fancy, it is in Tivoli that
the airy-fairy tissue is caught up in an incredible *pouf* bearing
no more resemblance to an ordinary amusement park than
Hamlet to Hercules. It is difficult to capture in prose the peculiar quality of these twenty acres in the heart of the city.
One buys a ticket and enters a turnstile gate quite as at Coney
Island or Southend. One sees walks and gardens and pavilions
and hears the voices of children and the crash of a distant
roller-coaster, but instead of being submerged by the pressure
and racket of vulgarity, one is wafted into a realm of innocence, and steps into a naïve vista like a pink-sashed little girl
or a blue-bowed little boy walking through a lace-paper frame
into the heart of a valentine. It is not remarkable that there
should be concert halls, dance halls, fashionable, semi-
fashionable, and not at all fashionable cafés; that there should
be a lake and boats and coloured lights playing on fountains,
and acrobats dancing on tight ropes over an open-air stage,
and somewhere the sound of a band and marching feet. What
is remarkable about Tivoli is that everyone—from the mil-
lionaire to the newsboy, from the professor to the laundress—
comes to it. A banker entertains a distinguished colleague
from abroad with dinner at Tivoli. A janitress brings her
sandwiches and buys a cup of coffee and spends her half-
holiday at Tivoli. Two million men, women, and children
from Copenhagen, from the Provinces, from all Europe pass
the turnstiles in the summer season, and all are so miracu-
lously transformed that rowdyism is as inconceivable as in
fairyland itself. Those sailor boys, on an evening's leave, are

apparently from Gilbert and Sullivan's good ship *Pinafore:* those Americans, ready for whoopee, are, without conscious volition, inducted from shrill excitement to happy gaiety. Young men and girls, strolling along the flowery walks or sitting side by side in an arbour, are friendly and frank, but some inexplicable potency mesmerizes licentiousness into romance. This Arcadian simplicity is the inimitable secret of Tivoli, but it offers one more tangible novelty, and that is its open-air pantomime theatre, unique in Europe, where an art which has been lost or altered elsewhere has been preserved through unbroken generations. Twice daily the curtain of the Peacock Theatre rolls back and a thousand or so people follow, engrossed, the dainty classic mimicry. Those in the front sit down, those far behind hire periscopes. All are motionless— the father with his little son on his shoulder, the grandmother leaning on her cane. Behind this great quiet audience there stands, with white ruff, cocked eyebrows, and red-painted mouth, for ever turned toward the Peacock Theatre, a bust of Niels Henrik Volkersen, for years the beloved Pierrot of Tivoli.

Casorti came trooping up from Italy nearly a hundred and fifty years ago, bringing with him Cassander and Columbine, Pierrot and Harlequin. They cried and laughed all over Europe, but when they reached Copenhagen they settled down for life—for more than any mortal life, for they have danced and pranced here ever since, the only place left in the mundane universe, apparently, where they are completely at home. Every now and then some new playwright tries his hand at the Peacock Theatre, but not very successfully. All Casorti's score of pantomimes follow each other in unwearying familiarity, every traditional gesture meticulously maintained. The agelessness of the characters seems, in a measure, to descend to the actors, for one Harlequin played on his eightieth birthday, and certain Columbines and Pierrots have frolicked for three generations of admirers.

And why not, in the enchanted garden of an enchanted city, where midnight is announced by a million comets and rockets rushing across the sky, and a million stars unhampered by astronomical name and position dance and disappear? The voice of the story-teller ceases, the covers of the Tivoli storybook are closed, and Prince and Pierrot and pastry-cook, in that fantastic juxtaposition possible only in a fairy-tale, pass out into the street.

To become acquainted with an old city, to pass beyond the fun of its external novelty and sink into its essential rhythm, is of profounder moment than making a new human acquaintance. For an old city, existing before and destined to live after anyone now moving within it, has a personality so rich that to come into response with it expands one's own personality. Individual lives have flung their energies, hopes, terrors, and laughter into this general life, and its aura is made up of emotions whose creators have their only mortal perpetuity in that aura.

Copenhagen is such a city. Waves of countless lives, tides of uncounted generations have beaten upon its spiritual shores, and one who has a listening ear can still hear those far vibrations. Meanwhile, the present crowding jocund inheritors surge through the streets, erect new buildings, perfect new inventions, and raise new statues. The bicycles scurry by, the towers glitter, and the sensible city of reality and the supersensible realm of fancy are united under one crown.

CHAPTER TWO

SOCIAL SECURITY THAT SECURES

THE towers topped with golden crowns, the streets sparkling with golden symbols, Tivoli closing its gates with a swirl of stars—these are merely illustrations of the fairy story.

A country which takes care of her old and of her young, of her sick and of her unemployed; where no one need go cold or hungry; where doctors and hospitals are at the service of whoever needs them—this is the modern fairy story.

The Constitution of Denmark rather naïvely forbids any Dane to starve. The Social Reform of Denmark—which stamps that country as one of the most enlightened in the world—goes further. No Dane should starve, but neither should his life be filled with fear: fear of sickness, of invalidity, of unemployment, of indigent old age.

The last enemy of all, the Bible says, is death. But certainly more people are terrified by the pain of helpless or poverty-stricken life than by the oblivion of death. To remove that terror, to give every man and woman an opportunity to prepare, and prepare adequately, for any exigency of the future, is the noble objective of Denmark's social legislation. (Not only to give them this opportunity but to force them to accept it, is perhaps more accurate.)

The laws concerning social insurance, poor relief, and their administration cover fifty years and ramify into tomes. The recent Social Reform is a codification of three Insurance Acts —one covering health insurance, invalidity, and old age pensions, the second covering unemployment insurance, and the third being a workmen's compensation law—and an Act regarding public assistance. The codification is far from brief. It is enormous and intricate and, furthermore, it is constantly being altered, modified, developed. But in spite of this, it is possible for the average visitor to, or reader about, Denmark to grasp the main outlines of the system.

The feature which is most immediately spectacular is the Old Age Pensions.

Apparently any sweet old woman or cross old man—disposition is not important—past sixty-five and below a certain income level, has merely to hold out a hand and receive a pension from the Government, payable in advance and monthly. After that they may live where they please, or move into a cheerful free hotel, which not only provides bed and board, medical and nursing attention, but laundry, entertainment, and a spot of pocket money. This is the impression given by strolling into the Raadhus in Copenhagen and watching the men and women—neat, respectable, with no air of pauperism about them—who are receiving their pensions. It is the impression gained by visiting one of the many Homes for the Aged which bear no relation to a dingy poorhouse such as used to be shoved into the wretchedest part of the city or the loneliest section of the village. A Home for the Aged in Denmark is a dignified building whose exterior is a credit to the community and whose interior is arranged not only to keep its occupants alive but comfortable and even happy. But although about one hundred thousand people are receiving aid under the Old Age Pension System, it must not be deduced therefrom that it is an extravagant free-for-all panacea paid for by juggling of public funds. The Old Age Pension System is the result of nearly ninety years' careful consideration, revision, and modification. The Danish Constitution of 1849 was the first step, and the Law of 1891 the second. While its object is to care humanely—even tenderly—for all aged men and women who need it, every effort is made to guard against its exploitation. It sometimes fails. Certain of the deserving are too proud to confess their need. Certain undeserving are cunning enough to get what is not intended for them. Those with whom the decisions rest may be susceptible to political pressure. Even in Denmark, as Bishop Palle mildly observed, "The people, unfortunately, are not so good as they ought to be." Miscarriages of justice are inevitable in any movement organized and executed by mortal man. But taken all in all, in its scrupulous and intelligent formulation and in its just application, the Danish Old Age Pension System, which is included in the Danish National Insurance Act, is worthy of respectful study.

Without entering into every technicality it may be broadly stated that an applicant for such a pension must be sixty-five years old, although in exceptional circumstances a Communal Council and the Minister for Social Affairs may grant it at sixty. An applicant must have taken out health insurance, or applied for such insurance. He must not have deliberately put himself in the economic status for receiving the pension, by irregular or extravagant living, or led a life offensive to public morals for five years previously. He must not have received aid under the Public Assistance Act in a manner that involved loss of franchise. He must have met certain requirements of paying the arrears of his health insurance if he had let it lapse and regaining his legal rights.

The pension consists of a certain basic sum which is reduced in proportion to the income of the person entitled to the pension but which may be supplemented by certain additions. These basic sums are different for different ages: different in the capital city, the towns, the rural districts, and to some extent they are regulated by the cost of living. Seven-twelfths of the cost of Old Age Pensions is paid by the Government and five-twelfths by the municipality of the person in question.

An idea of the amount of such a pension may be gained from the fact that the highest collective income for a sixty-five-year-old married couple, when both are receiving a pension, amounts to about 1720 kroner (about $430.00) annually in Copenhagen and in the rural areas 1185 kroner ($296.00).

There is also an Invalidity Pension for persons under the age of sixty-five who have health-insured themselves and whose earning capacity has been reduced to one-third of their normal earnings.

Those who are too infirm to live alone or cannot be placed out for private nursing are admitted to Homes for the Aged such as are erected by most of the boroughs and by many of the rural communes. The pensioner continues to receive his pension as long as his economic status—and for the invalidity pensioner his health—remains unchanged.

The Danes are a long-lived people. Unlike New York, which the cynic remarked had nothing old in it but the young men's faces, Copenhagen is abundantly supplied with spruce octogenarians and sibyls grown ample with fourscore years of generous eating. They are seen in the restaurants, applying themselves to their afternoon cakes and coffee and to sandwiches spread with lobster and caviare and cheese before which a younger and weaker-livered generation might quail. These are familiar and heartening figures. But indigent old age is another and a sadder business, and the most determined persiflage resolves itself into making the sorry best of it. It may be that Denmark treats its old age pensioners so well that they live longer than they otherwise would and so the problem, even if approximately solved, is prolonged. But in any case the question of Old Age Pensions is settled and while certain regulations may be altered the system is definitely accepted.

While Old Age Pensions are a free gift from the public, Invalidity Pensions are based on the same principle as the Health Insurance—that of "help to self-help."

There are 1650 Sick Clubs, as they are called, in the country, all separate units but all subject to State supervision. Each is supported partly by its members' contributions and partly by the State. While 77 per cent of the people apply voluntarily for membership in such a club, everyone over twenty-one is *required* to belong, if not as an active then as a passive member—a significant innovation in the history of health insurance. The latter membership is obtained at a lower fee and carries the privilege of becoming active, irrespective of age and health status in the future. The members, then, are obliged to support their Sick Club and their Sick Club is obliged to furnish its members with free hospital treatment; free medical aid, medicine, cash benefits, maternity benefits, and so forth. More than any other national system, as I. S. Falk points out in his recent book, *Security against Sickness,* Danish sickness insurance provides medical care rather than cash benefits.

A voluntary scheme of unemployment insurance which, however, receives assistance from public funds, is also in operation. It is interlocked with trade unions which require their members to be insured against unemployment. As about 85 per cent of all Danish workers are organized, a relatively complete system of insurance has been established without statutory compulsion.

Workmen's Compensation, on the other hand, is compulsory, the employers being responsible for the whole cost of the contribution. Since 1917 the Act has covered not only workers in all the trades, but all persons doing work for others.

The country has long had a complete system of municipal and county hospitals, and a good point from which to study them is Bispebjerg Hospital in Copenhagen. This tremendous institution, with its six pavilions connected above ground by gardens and terraces, and underground by seven kilometres of tiled corridors, with its two surgical and two medical departments, with its handsome equipment and cheerful appearance, is on a scale and of a character similar to the best private hospitals of lavish endowment. The maximum price a patient may pay in the Bispebjerg Hospital is 1 krone 20 öre (or less than 35 cents a day). Every type of service and medical care is given to the poor, without charge, at the cost of the municipality. Insured people have their fees paid by their insurance societies at a 50 per cent discount. Others pay their charges privately. The rich may come here as well as the poor, and many do because of the skilful surgeons and doctors, superior nursing and therapeutics. But the rich man cannot pay more than the stipulated 1 krone 20 öre, or demand any other kind of accommodation than the doctor recommends. Privacy depends not upon the patient's purse, but upon the doctor's decision as to the necessities of the case. Those who want special privileges and can pay for them are free to go to private hospitals and pay 12 kroner upward a day.

Besides the Bispebjerg there are eight other municipally owned hospitals in Copenhagen, and throughout Denmark one finds similar first-class institutions operated on the same principle and price scale. Hospital physicians are salaried officers, and this brings us to the system by which doctors are paid a fixed yearly salary.

Since 90 per cent of the people in Denmark over fourteen years of age carry health insurance, nearly all the physicians except the specialists engage in insurance practice. "With approximately 2000 such physicians there is one for each 870 insured persons (and their dependents). The total insurance expenditures for medical services rendered to insured persons by general practitioners ($2.19 per member) are equivalent to an assured income of approximately $1900.00 per physician."

Socialized medicine is under such discussion in the United States that it is pertinent to quote Mr. Falk's excellent summary of the system which has been highly successful in Denmark.

Medical service is provided by physicians working under agreements which are of two kinds. Outside of Copenhagen, the insurance institutions have no authority to select physicians; all physicians in good standing who report to the regional section of the Danish Medical Association that they are willing to serve, may be remunerated for services to insured persons. In Copenhagen, on the contrary, the doctors are engaged by the insurance societies. Physicians are remunerated either according to a fee schedule for the services they render or on a flat rate at so much per insured person per year (capitation fee). The total expenditures to physicians during a year are approximately equally divided between those who serve on an attendance and on a capitation basis. Special payment provisions are made for the care of chronic patients, for those requiring surgery, for night calls, travel charges, etc. When payment rests on a capitation basis, special payments are limited to very few services and are made according to an agreed fee schedule.

In Copenhagen, the patient does not have entirely—but he does have very substantial—free choice of doctor; the city is divided into three main districts and fifteen sub-districts, and he may choose among the local contract physicians in his main district. "Free choice" by the patient is limited, however, by the fact that no physician may accept more than 1500 persons as potential patients. In the provinces, the patient generally has free choice of all physicians in the town or within a radius of ten kilometers if the physicians are paid on a fee schedule, or he has entirely free choice of his physician for the coming year if they are paid on a capitation basis. Where the physician is paid on a capitation basis, the patient cannot as a rule change his doctor during the year except for good and sufficient cause.

There are no legal provisions to settle disputes between sickness funds and their members, but in practice such disputes are submitted to, and are settled by, the supervising governmental authorities. Disputes between patients and doctors are settled by hearings before the chairman of the local physicians' association and the officers of the fund, and appeals may be taken first to a joint medical and lay council, and, since 1929, may be carried to the Minister of Social Affairs.

Hospital care is provided in the local government hospitals and the cost is paid by the insurance funds at agreed rates. The hospitals are operated on high standards of quality and yet economically, so that this type of service is provided at comparatively small cost. Specialist services are often furnished under contracts of service between sickness societies and the specialists.

In regard to these specialists who do not engage in insurance work but must confine themselves to private practice: such a specialist must have, after graduation from the State Medical College, an interneship of one year, two years' practice as a physician outside his special field, and training in his special field for two or three years more. After that, he goes before a committee and is either accepted or rejected. This committee consists of a member of the medical faculty, a specialist practising in the same line as the applicant, the chief physician of the hospital, a physician in Copenhagen, a physician outside Copenhagen, and a representative from the association of younger physicians.

From all this it may be seen that public health, hospital, and private practitioners all work together efficiently. The expenditures for medical services paid from tax funds are approximately equal to those paid for medical benefits by insurance societies.

In spite of general popular acceptance, a few people still declare that pensions and benefits curse him who gives and him who takes, corrupting the former and demoralizing the latter. They deplore carrying the poor to the skies on flowery beds of ease, ignoring the fact that since the average labourer gives 10 per cent to 15 per cent of his income toward social insurance, he is not a passive recipient of bounty. A man of moderate income pays about 19 per cent of it in direct taxation.

While Denmark has carried Social Reform to such satisfactory conclusion, it does not follow that the same system would work equally well elsewhere. Denmark is very small. Relief administration is handled by local officials who are too well known in their neighbourhood to indulge in glaringly corrupt practices. Furthermore, Denmark has always had great respect for law. While there is political corruption, it is at a minimum; court decisions penalize abuses heavily, even sentencing the offenders to jail.

Neither has Denmark always been the model state which today attracts economists and students of social betterment from the perplexed countries of the world. In *Pelle the Conqueror*—one of the pieces of Danish fiction best known to English readers—Martin Andersen Nexö paints a Denmark of the latter nineteenth century quite different from that of the present twentieth.

This prodigious novel is far more than the life of the single individual whose story it is. Pelle as the doughty, dirty little lad, the son of a labourer on a farm in Bornholm; Pelle the adolescent, miserable, rollicking shoemaker's apprentice in the town; Pelle the courageous champion of the downtrodden in Copenhagen; and finally Pelle the founder of a garden city for his fellow-workers whose poverty he has so bitterly shared, is indeed a convincing and engaging personality, but it is the social struggle and the growth of the labour movement in Denmark, the background for both the country and the city scenes, which give Nexö's novel its permanent significance.

The enormous length of the book, about eighteen hundred

closely printed pages, makes it rather a mouthful for the English reading public even in this day of gigantesque "best sellers." But there is no other volume which will limn for the foreigner such pictures of the farm and water front, of the foul alleys and cruel docks of the city half a century ago. To peruse its many hundred pages is to penetrate slowly, methodically, and without benefit of expurgation into the dark workshops where the submerged worked—when there was work; into the wretched garrets and basements where they lived—when there was food to live on.

These things have changed. Even the persuasive Martin Andersen Nexö who, as an avowed Communist, is still vigorously exposing abuses and social discrepancies and inveighing against the distribution of wealth in his native land, admits improvement. But the era of slums and exploitation of the labourer on the farm and in the factory is past. The Denmark of fragrant meadows and sun-flecked beech woods, described with equal poignance, still exists and there still exist—the book's enduring distinction—the tragedies and comedies of a multitude of small lives: philosophies and resignations of many humble souls. Such stories will be lived in tears and smiles for a long time to come, even in a land of national insurance and public assistance: even in a country which has worked out one of the most humane programmes of social security that the world has ever contrived.

The thatch-roofed farm buildings contain the home for the family, barn for the live stock, and winter food for them all.

ALLEGHENY COLLEGE LIBRARY

To step into a peasant farmhouse is to step into an atmosphere of
thrift and family affection.

ALLEGHENY COLLEGE LIBRARY

The storks which winter in South Africa fly back to Ribe every
spring and are welcomed as symbols of peace.

ALLEGHENY COLLEGE LIBRARY

There is a milch cow for every other person in Denmark. On a large estate, each of the dozen milkmaids milks eighteen cows night and morning.

ALLEGHENY COLLEGE LIBRARY

Hindsgavl, headquarters of the Norden Club, was once a private château where, in 1814, the Treaty of Kiel was signed.

ALLEGHENY COLLEGE LIBRARY

Small towns accept in their old age the same affection and flattery
they did not question in their youth.

ALLEGHENY COLLEGE LIBRARY

PART II

Out of the Earth

CHAPTER ONE

THE PLANTED FIELDS

THE crowded buildings and irregular streets of the city unravel into the wide boulevards and modernistic apartment houses, parks and playgrounds of the outskirts, into the tree-shaded avenues and detached villas of the suburbs, into the undulating planted fields and half-timbered white farmhouses of the country. There is no abrupt transition. There is no ring of slums: there are no dumps and derelicts around Copenhagen or any Danish city, for that matter. The country grows up to the town as naturally as the sea sands are moulded into the dunes, as softly as clouds roll into cloud banks. Although Denmark has its forests, heaths, and moors, as we journey through South Zealand its total impression is of a succession of fields of grain, gardens, meadows and grazing land, not in chequerboard regularity but in a recurrent rhythmical pattern, built up on a system of modulated contours and colours from which everything sharp and ugly was long ago gently dissolved.

Through such a countryside runs the road to Falster, and although this highway bears (between Copenhagen and Roskilde) more traffic than any other in Denmark, although the

State Railway is not far away and the popular beaches are dotted by tent settlements and week-end cabins, all this human animation seems but a bright line between the larger calm of the sky and the deeper quiet of the fields.

Roskilde, Ringsted, and Sorö—we leave their past history and present busyness for another day. Kjöge shall be our first stop this morning and our introduction to those ancient buildings which have been preserved with such care and in such numbers throughout all Denmark as to infuse this progressive and modern country with the unpurchasable grace of antiquity.

Not that there are many towns in Denmark where one may see so many buildings of such age—1527 is over the door of one house and the Church of St. Nicolaj dates from 1324—or of such handsome proportions as those in Kjöge. These two-story dwellings with their elaborately carved oak beams, hard, heavy, and black as iron, belonged to men of importance four centuries ago. And from those times until today lace curtains have hung at the casement windows: housewives have bustled through the low-ceilinged rooms, and children have played, as they are playing now, in the enclosed courtyards. For Kjöge is not a show place. It confines its static exhibits to a museum appropriately housed in an old Spinning Court and concerns itself with manufacturing rubber goods and pigment for paint. With Danish sentiment it cherishes its architectural heirlooms; with Danish common sense it utilizes them: as the fertile meadow yonder has been ploughed, sowed, and reaped for half a thousand years, so has Kjöge been lived in and loved. Life has been passed from one generation to the next as those oak-timbered buildings have belonged to each succeeding generation for the span of its existence. This sense of continuity, of obligation to the past and duty to the future, is a common-place to the old nations of Europe. Visitors from rawer and less organized countries ponder on it and are sobered.

The cobbled streets of Kjöge, and Kjöge Bay, where Niels Juel won the great naval battle over Sweden in 1677, give place to the open fields—golden fields of wheat, rosy fields of clover. The two-story red brick houses of Kjöge give place to one-story whitewashed farmhouses whose two or three wings embrace a courtyard, whose thatched roofs unite them in brown intimacy to the brown earth, and whose whole prosperous, well-kept air proclaims the independent farmer, proud and justly proud of his homestead and his land.

Green fields, red cows, and a white farmhouse; yellow fields, white fowls, and a white farmhouse; an acre of purple cabbages and a red-tiled church; a field dashed with scarlet poppies; an open pasture tranquil with bovine groups; more fields and more red cows and the turning sails of a windmill high set on a distant flat terrain; more fields and more red cows, and at irregular but fairly frequent intervals that low white group of buildings whose proportions never fail to delight the eye and whose series of thatched roofs confine the home for the family, the barn for the live stock, and the winter food for them all.

And just as one becomes contentedly convinced that all Denmark is an unbroken sweep of field and farm, and man's one function is to cultivate the earth, the spires of Vallö lift above the trees and Vallö Castle rises above its moat with towers and drawbridge and stone-carved entrance gate. Swans drift above their own reflections. Lawns, parks, and flower gardens fall away in tiers and terraces. All is stately, rich, and proud, for here sisters, daughters, and kinswomen of noble families are housed and served as splendidly as princesses in any fairy-tale.

Vallö has sheltered Kings and Queens, has been passed back and forth between noble families, and has served as a stage for intrigue and romance for six hundred years. (The oldest document connected with it—a deed of gift from King Christopher —dates from the beginning of the fourteenth century.) But its present status was determined when Queen Sophie founded the Royal Vallö Stift (1737). By its charter, confirmed by the King, the Abbess must be of royal birth, the Deaconesses descended from Counts, and the Stifts Frökner of noble descent. Although these qualifications have been somewhat revised in two centuries, the Vallö Dames are still "Their Graces" and their protectresses are still the Queens and Dowager Queens of Denmark. And its endowment, as well as its lands and forests, have kept Vallö not only an aristocratic but an immensely wealthy concern. "Their Graces" live in style. Each has her suite and staff of servants and runs an independent household as well as enjoying the privileges of parks and gardens.

One must not confuse such an institution with a convent or an old ladies' home. The entrance applications for daughters of noble families are sometimes made out at birth with an entrance fee of 4000 kroner, and once safely within "this great house with the two big towers," as the legend over the gateway describes it, they are assured until their deaths of an abode not only safe but sumptuous.

Isak Dinesen in "The Monkey" suggests the atmosphere of this hostel peopled with noble ladies living so freely and so elegantly, although the subject matter of the story, like that of most of the malodorous, fantastically painted deep-sea fruit of *Seven Gothic Tales,* leaves the reader drugged and drowsy rather than refreshed.

Vallö is worth a detour, not only because it is a superb example of Renaissance architecture but because, with it, we begin to realize that there are castles as well as cottages in this rolling countryside, many castles and of vast dimensions, surrounded by parks and private forests and tenant farmers. Who said Denmark was a land of peasants, each tilling his own few acres?

There are still great estates in Denmark—a surprising number of them: moated manor-houses and turreted castles accent the landscape, and aristocratic life maintains its spaciousness beside bucolic thrift. But the owners of the large estates no longer exploit the peasants as they did in former centuries when the villenage system compelled the tenants to render assistance in the cultivation of the lords' lands. The Danish peasant, who until the last two decades of the eighteenth century was as wretched, as debt-ridden and impotent as his brothers throughout Europe, is now the economic bulwark of the country, a vital legislative power, and justly credited for his share in placing Denmark in the forefront of the agricultural countries of the world. This extraordinary readjustment of the whole system of land tenure—a change greater than any wrought in France by the Revolution—was accomplished in Denmark without bloodshed. It was accomplished by legislation, co-operation, and education. The last two demand—each of them —a chapter. The former, which has been a rational and fore-sighted progression, may be briefly outlined.

The established social order of autocratic idleness for the minority of the human family, and slaving penury for the majority, was until fairly recently accepted as inevitable in Denmark as in other European countries. The peasant, as a rule, was a tenant holding his farm on uncertain terms, ignorant, with primitive tools, at the mercy of his overlord, fettered by the military system, by ecclesiastical tithes, by villenage, and, last but not least, by "community of cultivation," which meant that all the farmers in a given area had to sow the same crop on the same day. The land of each tenant was not a compact area, but composed of strips scattered all over the three great fields into which the arable land was divided for purposes of crop rotation. These chains kept the male members of the rural population imprisoned, practically for life, on the estate where they were born.

The reform legislation—stamping Denmark as a social pioneer—began in 1769 with an act prohibiting free yeoman farmers from merging their properties into adjoining estates, and was followed by another forbidding the division of farms into lots too small to provide a living for one family. These measures were indicative of a succession of laws, all of them shaped to preserve the small and medium-sized farm and to encourage independent ownership. Villenage was abolished in 1788. Credit associations were founded (1851) as co-operatives of property owners seeking loans. Special benefits were granted by the State (1880) to credit unions assisting small owners in purchasing and developing their land.

The succeeding years are marked by a steady progression of laws framed, with increasing generosity, to increase the number of small holdings. The State granted money for loans from 1899 and defined, with great care, the conditions on which candidates are admitted to such tenures. Properties are divided into manors, farms, and small holdings, and the size of the last-named determined. In 1919, by a sensational enactment, most of the glebe land was sold and divided into small holdings, and the feudal lands, entailed estates, and feoffments converted into free property by their paying a certain sum of money to the State. Furthermore, these great properties were obliged to give up a certain proportion of their land (for compensation set by the State) and this land was to be used to establish small holdings. In districts where the demand for land could not be satisfied by such arrangement, the Minister of Agriculture might purchase, parcel out, and sell land.

This entire policy of land reform—consistently increasing the number of small holdings and shearing down the power and extent of large estates—was carried on constructively and without violence or haste and in the face of many difficulties. The large landowners were entitled to justice and had to be both supervised and controlled.

Today Denmark has the most efficient small farmers in the world, and 92 per cent of the agricultural holdings are cultivated by their owners, but they are not so many and they are not so autocratic as they were. There are pig-headed small farmers, but they are not so pig-headed as they were and they are more numerous. Vallö is a significant spot on which to stand and trace back through a perspective of one hundred and seventy years the legislative skeleton beneath the firm flesh of present-day Denmark.

The road between Vallö and Naestved passes many a park-like meadow where a single superb oak recalls that in the old days when nobles had to pay a higher tax for cultivated land than for woodland, they often left one tree in an open field,

thus technically bringing it under the classification of "forest"
—for which subterfuge all lovers of beautiful landscape must
thank them.

Naestved, which celebrated its eight hundredth anniver-
sary in 1935, is frankly proud of its house with Christ and the
Twelve Apostles carved on the thirteen front standard timbers,
of its antique bridge and manors and back streets of medieval
narrowness: these honourable relics are preserved meticulously and displayed with affection. But Naestved does not rest
upon its past. It has a paper mill and a ceramic factory. There
are glass works near by, a college for young women, and one
of the best boys' schools in Denmark, Herlufsholm. And when
necessary they reverently and sensibly move the powdered
bones from the crypt of the church to install steam heat. In
fact, so well kept, so quickly repaired are the buildings
throughout all Denmark, it is hard to realize that the country, although it has never been occupied by any foreign force,
has had its share of vandalous invasion. The Swedes, coming
down from the north, stabled their horses in the church in
Kjöge. The Germans, coming up from the south, did full share
of damage in Jutland. The Spaniards burnt the castle at Kold-
ing, and Lord Nelson, commanding the British fleet, bombarded Copenhagen and knocked the spire off the Frue Kirke.
The red cock of fire has crowed many times over Copenhagen,
time and water have taken their toll, and yet the only ruin one
can see in the capital today is the few square metres of Jarmer's
Taarn (Tower).

The medieval spires, the modern chimneys of Naestved fade
behind us as we travel on through the closely cultivated
countryside, along tree-shaded, well-kept roads, past old cottages as fresh as new, past new cottages as pleasing as the old.

At Praestö we glimpse the sea and at Kallehave take the ferry to Möen.

The island of Möen—like the two others of Falster and Lolland near by—while separated from the larger Zealand, is at one with it agriculturally and socially. While it cannot be said that here the ground is more uninterruptedly cultivated—for there is no chip or crack in the enamelled green of Zealand— yet on this more southerly island the wheat and oats are standing higher and the yellow broom on the hillsides bears a larger blossom. On the island of Möen the fields of sugar beets extend like verdant seas, the haystacks and strawstacks are big as barns, and the houses behind the clipped hedges and trimmed trees were apparently all whitewashed yesterday afternoon and the doors and window frames were painted in contrasting colours this morning.

Of course, we know we are here to admire the chalk cliffs, for these abrupt white bluffs sliced sheerly to the sea are unique in a country of modest altitudes. But we are in no haste to leave behind these fields and farms and windmills, each house so like its neighbour, each one differentiated by some individual detail of cornice or corner, each church with its Gothic corbie-stepped gables so like the one just passed, and each one a delight.

As in every place which cools its heels and waits for the ferry, Möen has acquired a philosophy of not hurrying. The people saunter down the streets, the bicyclists take their time, the plough horses pace slowly over the rich earth. Someone must get up early to keep all these lace curtains starched, to water all those pelargoniums and geraniums on the window sills, to polish up the door knobs, to sweep the garden walks (and to sweep the grass after it is cut, according to tidy custom), to say

nothing of weeding and thinning these acres of sugar beets.
But despite these evidences of bustle, no bustle is evident. Two
girls lean over a bridge, a mother pushes a pram, a man smokes
his pipe on a bench against the currant bushes.

> "Rest, rest, a perfect rest,
> Shed over brow and breast,
> Her face is toward the west—the purple land."

Such comparison is not strictly accurate, as anyone must
admit after clambering the paths that zigzag up and down the
chalk cliffs, looking down on the blue water far below, and
out upon other cliffs, after wandering through beech woods
and along the strand and learning the names and listening to
the legends that are associated with the various fantastic con-
formations. Möen has its castle and its Viking graves, its museum, churches, hotels, and pensions—everything to ensure its
resort popularity. It makes the most of these advantages, but
with Danish common sense continues to plant sugar beets,
raise cows, and cut hay, since summer flowers bloom for a few
months only and thrift is evergreen throughout the year.

The longest bridge in Europe, carrying trains and traffic to
Germany, uses as its final span the small island of Falster. Falster and its neighbour Lolland, yoked together by a little
bridge, are both flat as the proverbial flounder and both possessed of a clayey soil which, when properly worked, is as fertile as any in all Denmark—a fact which early attracted to
them proprietors of great estates.

Despite the laws of disentailment and despite the heavy
taxes and increasingly drastic legislation, there are still a sufficient number of castles and manors left on these two islands
to serve as contrast to the small and medium-sized farms and

to serve, too, as a point from which to study not only the free-hold farm but also the freehold farmer—he who, a short while ago, was a labourer on the big estate.

Neither could there be a more agreeable place to make a survey of the agricultural achievements, both in scientific farming and co-operation, which make Denmark the marvel of the world.

Whoever thinks this democratic kingdom is entirely popu-lated with simple peasants or prosperous bourgeoisie has never stepped into the lofty entrance hall of an aristocratic estate with its swords, mirrors, and marble floor, its liveried men servants and waiting, white-capped maids; has never passed from that entrance hall into the apparently endless series of rooms beyond—rooms in which the portraits, statues, and costly furnishings accumulated through generations are merely a background for happy living. In such a house par-ents, children, tutors, relatives, guests, pets, servants, move in their natural orbits. Between such neighbouring houses the social intercourse of dinners, cards, tennis, hunting, and sailing continues in the best tradition of country life. Such an estab-lishment, in which hospitality is an art, tradition an instinct, and elegance the handmaid to comfort, is less formal than its counterpart in England, more placid than in America, more generous than in France. But a visitor from any of these coun-tries would, amid its manners, appointments, and customs, feel immediately at home. If he should stay long enough, however, to stroll beyond the lawns and park, the house garden, pleasure ponds, and riding ring, he would discover that this is as unlike an English estate, which derives its income chiefly from its rents, as it is unlike one in America which is a luxury or hobby of a man who earns his money in Wall Street. A Danish estate

of, say, four thousand acres is a practical working proposition
deriving its income from its fourteen hundred acres of woodland, from its two hundred and forty acres of beets (which are
converted into sugar at a near-by factory), from its two hundred cows whose milk is sent to a condensed milk factory, from
its hundred and fifty pigs. Fourteen hundred acres are divided
into twelve fields—sugar beets, barley, wheat, oats, seed sugar
beets, Italian ray grass, white clover, and so forth—all of them
ditched, drained, cultivated, sown, harvested with the best
modern machinery according to the best proved methods,
whether these latter happen to be ancient or modern. Thus the
dozen milkmaids who, night and morning, arrive in high rubber boots on bicycles to milk, each of them, eighteen cows,
milk them by hand just as Mrs. Noah did in the Ark with her
one cow because on this particular estate hand milking is believed to be the best. But the milk is cooled by the newest cool-
ing machine and handled as scrupulously as in a laboratory.
There is the same contrast up nearer the great house where all
this activity centres. The blacksmith shoes the forty working
horses and the half-dozen saddle horses, but can also weld a
bolt for the electric refrigerator. The carpenter repairs the
wooden laundry tub five feet across and also tinkers with the
radio. There are machines for chopping and mixing and mash-
ing fodder and for spraying whitewash. But the slaughter
house, smoke house, and salting house hark back to the days
before machinery. Here, controlled by the overseer, who has
his private quarters, and by the book-keeper, with his office,
house, and garden, is a self-contained village almost as complete as in medieval days, supporting about three hundred
people. And the owner of it, while by no means despising a
season of shooting in his private forest in the autumn, or a trip

to Paris in the winter, or a continuous house party in the
summer, is a practical and scientific agriculturist.

This much one may see by strolling beyond the sixty acres
dedicated to the kennels, conservatories, kitchen gardens,
orchards, and poultry yards which supply the household needs,
and investigating, further afield, the piggeries, the stables for
the work-horses, the cow barns, and all the vast housing and
machinery dedicated to the farm rather than to the family.
The sound of the farm bell, the distant glint of a reaper in the
fields, the air of busy routine, while not intruding upon the
gaieties in the big house, give it dignity and a *raison d'être*
which can never be simulated in a country place which is
merely, like so many luxurious American estates, a summer resort for the family, or, like many great English ones, an agreeable free hotel for social equals.

Such a stroll and such observations might lead a foreigner
to declare that in Denmark the ideal has been attained. What
more could any man desire than to be the owner of such a well-
functioning, prodigious farm and the master of such a splendid
and friendly home? And is not such an estate an ornament to
Denmark, a repository for its culture as well as a mainstay of
its economical life? And to these questions he is astonished to
receive a gloomy response. The owner tells him that the farm
does not pay as it once did and as it should; that legislation
works to the advantage of owners of four, forty, or four hundred acres but not to the owner of four thousand; that labour
is difficult—and increasingly so—to get. Two hundred cows
must be milked morning and night, and women who can milk
twelve to eighteen cows twice a day are not so easy to come by
and not so content with their weekly seven kroner as once
they were. It seems men prefer to work in their own fields

rather than be labourers in another's, or they prefer to go to the city. It seems, too, that the industrial party and the agricultural party disagree politically about certain matters of export and import, and that present legislation is more favourable to the factory worker than to the farmer. And, finally, it seems that taxes are so disproportionately high for the large landowner that he prognosticates his ultimate annihilation and says that Denmark will soon belong entirely to the small farmer who, with his family, does all the work of the farm, or to the medium-sized owner who, even with a few assistants, is himself a toiler.

Plainly the time has come when the foreigner, if he wishes to understand the basic facts upon which Danish prosperity rests at the present time, must take a more careful look at the small and medium-sized farm.

CHAPTER TWO

THE FARMER AND CO-OPERATION

THE Danish farmer steps out from his half-timbered, thatch-roofed barn which is an ell of his half-timbered, thatch-roofed house, trundling before him the big stoppered cans which hold the morning's milking. He leaves these cans by the front gate and in the course of the morning a man comes around with a cart or a lorry, picks them up and carries them to the near-by co-operative dairy—a spotless laboratory built on a proved standardized plan and operated by electricity, where the milk is weighed, measured, tested for bacteria and fat content, classified, and credited to the farmer's account. The skimmed milk which is not needed is poured back into the cans and returned to the farmer, who feeds it to his pigs. The farmer has nothing to do with the separating of the cream, the pasteurizing of the milk, with butter or cheese making. He merely produces so much milk and gets paid for it according to its classified value, obtaining for his comparatively small output the same price as that paid to the large farms, his income being in direct ratio to his intelligence in feeding and caring for his stock.

This same farmer hands his eggs over to a local egg-collecting centre from which they are gathered in by the Danish Co-operative Egg Export. Here they are candled, weighed, graded and stamped according to size and colour, and shipped to England—fifty-six million score in 1936—by any of twenty ships which scurry back and forth between Esbjerg and Harwich or Copenhagen and London, and the farmer receives the current price.

When he has decided which little pig should go to market, it is called for, transported to the co-operative slaughtery, and converted into bacon and ham, practically all of the former and 62 per cent of the latter being exported to England.

If he wants to export cattle, he may join any of the fifteen cattle societies which handle about 40 per cent of all the cattle export.

The sugar beets which take 10 per cent of the root area go to a sugar beet factory where there is enough sugar manufactured to make importation of it unnecessary. The sugar beet pulp is used for fodder.

The same system is applied even to hens and chickens, one and a half million of which went to co-operative slaughteries last year.

From all this it may be seen that the Danish farmer, assured of his market and the transportation of his produce to it, its processing there and its export, need not puzzle his head about the rate of foreign exchange, the problems of middlemen or shipping, but is free to devote his entire attention to farming. If he is efficient he gets top prices. If he is not efficient he has only himself to blame. For every process, from the cultivation of the soil to the smallest detail of feeding and breeding live stock, has been accurately worked out and the facts and figures are easily accessible.

Now, of course, there are efficient farmers in Asia, Africa, Australia, and America. Today the principles of scientific farming are understood all over the world. And equally, of course, in all the Scandinavian countries co-operative buying, selling, and manufacturing are widely practised. But nowhere on the globe have co-operation and agriculture been so remarkably united and applied with such scope and minuteness as in Denmark. The small farmer—who has from ten to fourteen acres, four cows, two horses, and three pigs and, with his family, does all his own work; the medium-sized farmer, with seventy acres, twenty-five cows, twenty-eight pigs, and four men labourers in the fields and a maid in the kitchen; the large estate owner, with four thousand acres and two hundred labourers—practically all are co-operators, although the large estate owners less generally than the others. Agricultural co-operation needs neither argument nor subsidy in Denmark. The small farmer knows that sixty years ago twice as much was paid for butter from manor farms as for that from little farms, and the former only was considered good enough for export. The manor farms always won the butter prizes at exhibitions. Inside thirty years the co-operative dairies were making a clean sweep of all the silver prizes and winning two hundred and two out of two hundred and six bronze medals.

The tall chimney of the co-operative dairy, seen in practically every town and hamlet, makes this the most conspicuous of the organizations: the first one was established in 1882 and now they deal with 90 per cent of all the milk of Denmark and one-third of the butter turnover of the world. The co-operative bacon factories dating from 1887 follow close, taking care of 84 per cent of all the killings. Connected with these are the Joint Sales Company, the Danish Bacon Company in

London, and all the factories organized in the Union of Danish Co-operative Bacon Factories. Whoever has heard an expert discourse on the fine bones, the well-developed hams, the white meat, the thin back and thick stomach of the ideal hog; on the consistence, colour, aroma, and flavour of perfect bacon; of the arrangements and temperatures of a proper sty, realizes there are more things involved than are dreamed of in any Horatio's philosophy.

Agricultural co-operation does not confine itself to selling. A cow must not only be milked but must be fed. A field must not only be planted and reaped but must be fertilized. And 67 per cent of the total net imports of feeding stuffs and 36 per cent of the imported artificial manures are handled by co-operative purchase societies. The seed growers—most of them large-scale farmers—have organized into a society of three thousand four hundred members.

There are several reasons for this extraordinary specialization of the co-operative system: the geographical position of Denmark—near an industrial England needing dairy products, the increase of small farmers and their determination to make their living from the soil, the development of technical knowledge and agricultural machinery, and finally the character and ability of the Danish peasant. All of these factors have been appreciated. The United Kingdom (1934) supplied 30.1 per cent of Denmark's imports and took 60 per cent of Denmark's exports, of which the greater part was agricultural produce. The increase of small independent farmers was due partly to the constructive legislation described in the last chapter, while the education and character of the Danish peasant will be explained in the chapter following. As for the development of technical knowledge, this, of course, found its first followers on the large estates, as they were the only ones that could afford to buy and try the swing plough and the scarifier, to drain the land, to experiment with new forms of cultivation and new field plants, and to adopt methods for improving breeds of cattle. The big landowners were pioneers in agricultural theory, and clergymen, manufacturers, and merchants formed with them the first agricultural societies. But now the smallest farmer, through co-operation, can have the advantage of the best machinery, and he has been educated to understand the most advanced methods, so that crops have increased 150 per cent in fifty years.

Today agriculture in Denmark is practically an industry and a farm may be compared to a factory.

The cows are machines, unceasingly converting their prescribed provender into milk, while, without loss of motion or material, their precious waste is returned to the earth to fertilize more provender. A cow barn hums with the sound of these munching, milking, mooing machines, each one yielding about three thousand kilos of milk annually and getting —besides her hay and beet pulp—one pound of cattle cake for every two and a half pounds of milk she gives, quite like a motor being automatically given so much gasolene for so many revolutions, or a book being advertised by its publisher in ratio to its sales. It must be admitted, where all living creatures are humanely, even affectionately treated, that the cow has more the status of a machine than an animal.

Although she grazes in the field all summer and is even milked outdoors, during the entire winter she is stalled with only enough bodily freedom to lie down and stand up. Both she and her quarters are kept clean—no one need cry Woe! Woe! to the Danish farmer for making clean the outside of the cup and the platter and leaving the inside foul, for the ubiquitous whitewash is not spared; but any aspirations she may have beyond mere food and sanitation are unkindly ignored. Her infant calf is removed from her twenty-four hours after it is born—the reason one never sees a calf in the fields and sees so much veal on the menus—quite as if it were a mere bolt of finished material lifted from the loom.

If the cow is a machine, the pig is raw material. Skimmed milk and barley flowing down eight million gullets in automatic time cycle, according to proved regulation, are transformed into eight million carcasses as absolutely uniform in size, shape, and weight as so many drops of water.

One could carry the mechanical comparison further and say that the fields and gardens are departments of the factory. Nothing is left to chance on a Danish farm. If one hundred seed potatoes are planted in a row, one hundred potato plants should be blooming and mature at the appointed time. If one is lacking, the vacant spot is a wordless witness that the farmer has failed to do what he should do and what he knows how to do.

Denmark long ago realized that since her small area makes quantity production impossible, her economic life depends upon quality production—a principle which she has carried out in every line of endeavour. Although technical excellence and a high standard are valued in industry as in agriculture, they are perhaps more visually apparent in the latter, where so many and such healthy animals give colour to a landscape which is like a park when it is not like a garden.

But if Danish agriculture may be considered an industry, and a barn and field a factory, it would be a mistake to think of the Danish home as standardized. To stop at one of the little farmhouses, as intimate to the ground as a beehive, where the grandmother is knitting by the window and the children are clattering around in their wooden shoes, is to step into an atmosphere of thrift and family affection which cheerily defies regimentation. In spite of the tasks that have been done, that are being done, and that must continue to be done all day and every day, there seems to be time for the enjoyment of life. The mother, washing out the big milk cans, is not too busy to pick up her baby and hug it, or too preoccupied to put a bouquet of flowers on the table, or toss a spool for a black-and-white kitten to scamper after. The father, working in the fields, has obviously not been too busy to work also in the flower beds near the house; not too poor to feed the dog who wags his tail and grins at everyone. It is impossible to see these hundreds of humble farms without realizing that each one represents ownership and hard work and parenthood and affection—the fundamental human needs finding fundamental satisfaction. The normal ambition of the man to achieve independence is encouraged by State and school. The woman's house pride is sinfully fanned by contests and various "better homes and gardens" organizations. And communism, flourishing most readily on tenant soil or on none at all, finds scant foothold in a kingdom of independent landowners.

The newer farmhouse—as, for instance, one built since 1919 on land taken from an entailed estate—is equally heartening. It is of white stucco, with a red-tiled, snub-nosed roof in accordance with the pleasing popular style. Its interior may not be as quaint as that of its hundred-year-old neighbour, but the telephone, radio, and electric stove doubtless compensate to the woman of the house. The threshing machine and tractor, held in common with two or three neighbours, and the

five bicycles in the barn indicate that the man is also well established. Such a farmer on such a farm, built on former fiefs, entailed properties, and feoffments, has paid no purchase sum for
his land, but he pays interest to the State on its value as
appraised from time to time for the purpose of levying the
ground tax, and he holds this land with all the essential rights
of an owner. In accordance with the Act of 1919, with later
amendments, 5110 farmers have been established between
1920 and 1934, whereas 15,607 small holdings according to the
earlier legislation dating back to 1899 have been created between 1900 and 1934.

Not only the Government and his own co-operative societies stand ready to help the farmer, but Small Holders' Associations—there are 1243 of these—and Farmers' Associations—
there are 136 of these—and the Royal Agricultural Society
all work for the improvement and development of agriculture. The Agricultural Council represents agricultural interests in dealing with the Government, with foreign countries, and with other Danish industries. Besides all of these,
there are breeding societies and breeding centres and control
societies, agricultural awards and journals and contests and
live stock shows. And there are the cattle fairs.

A Danish cattle fair is an Elysian farm yard. Here under the
open sky stand rows of trumpeting stallions, broad as they are
long and, like all Danish animals, stuffed to bursting and cur-
ried and combed until they shine like suns. Here are great
sows as pink as roses and nuzzling piglets as pink as rosebuds.
Here are prodigious bulls unconcerned about their waist lines,
and red cows, bred for milk, not for meat: white cows, white
sheep, white poultry, surrounded by booths with exhibits,
models, charts, and information for making the bulls bigger,

the pigs pinker, and the cows milkier, holding ever before the latter the bovine champion who produced over a thousand pounds of butter in a year.

In this cheerful jostle of men and animals the farmers gather and, true to farmers' tradition the world over, bewail the difficulties and insufficient remuneration of their labours.

They are well dressed, well fed, and well educated, these Danish farmers, and they are able not only to make a living but to save, even on so small a property as ten acres. And why not, with the Government standing behind them with loans, and England standing before them in an illimitable vista of breakfast tables clamouring for bacon and eggs and butter, and their own co-operative organizations standing in their convenient midst transporting milk to dairy, and pig to slaughtery, and casks of butter and crates of eggs to waiting ships?

They are well dressed, well fed, well educated, and all of them—those who own twelve acres and those who own twelve hundred—are shaking their heads mournfully and declaring that at the present prices for dairy products they cannot live. They complain that the industrial party by refusing to import more goods from Germany makes it impossible for the farmer to export more of his products to Germany. They complain that if the heath land continues to be reclaimed and turned into agricultural areas, there will be over-production and prices will drop. They complain that Denmark provides merely 30 per cent of the world's trade in butter, 60 per cent of its bacon, and 10 per cent of its eggs, and, although it would be easy to raise more, there is no use doing so since it cannot be exported. They complain that the United States does not take any of their dairy produce—does not need it—and therefore Denmark cannot import motor cars from the United

States, and they dearly love American cars. Some argue that they should produce less milk and thereby raise the price. Others argue that they should raise fewer cows which would produce more milk since, they explain, milk production is merely a matter of feeding (although the simple-minded might believe that there was a limit both to what an animal can consume and what she can produce).

However, they all agree that the farmer cannot make a living under present conditions and that the industrial worker is unfairly favoured by legislation. So they take a glass of beer together, watch the horse races awhile, and then bicycle home to the farmhouse sparkling white behind the hawthorn hedge, with its flowers about the door-step and its fields and gardens spread neatly out on every side. The wife has milked the cows, the children have fed the pigs and poultry on the little farm, and the labourers have attended to these matters on the medium-sized farm.

But on little or medium or big farm, under thatched roof or tiled roof, after a hearty supper they all listen to the radio, or study the bulletins they have brought back from the fair, or read their co-operative journals, and finally drop asleep under their eiderdown bed covers, cheerfully convinced that the Danish farmer has a hard time of it.

CHAPTER THREE

THE FARMER
AND HIS FOLK HIGH SCHOOL

TO think of Denmark merely as a practical, fertile country, producing butter and eggs for England, is to read the notes and not hear the music. For Denmark's health and happiness are not constituted of component parts of good soil, good luck, and good management. They spring from a profounder source and are the visible manifestation of an aspiration more Utopian than utilitarian.

When, in the seventies and early eighties of the last century, Danish agriculture was hard hit by foreign competition in the grain markets of Europe, Denmark changed with an unexpected mobility and intelligence from the export of wheat to that of butter and bacon. The Danish peasant, stubborn and superstitious, had by some miracle become a progressive independent farmer able to adjust himself to new conditions, to establish standards of dairy products so excellent and so uniform that the country was saved and the rest of the world was dumbfounded.

This salvation of Denmark was due to the transformation

of a sullen peasantry, incapable of concerted action, into a farmer class heartily and astutely co-operative. This was based upon a logical process of education, and upon this process hang all the law and—in this case—the profits.

It was Nicolaj Frederik Severin Grundtvig (1783–1872) who passionately preached that if a man—even a peasant—seeks first the Kingdom of Heaven all other things will be added to him. And his contemporaries received this evangel, some with scepticism and some with the devotion that it had received at its first pronouncement seventeen hundred years previously.

Grundtvig, who was a theologian and a poet, believed—really believed—that an eager heart and a desire for wisdom are the greatest things in the world. He really believed that although these things might be hidden from the wise and prudent, they might be revealed to the simple. He really believed that if a whole nation—even the educated and the aristocratic—should become liberal in outlook and sensitive in spirit that, while its reward would be the enrichment of its inner life, the tangible blessings would also follow.

When, as an indigent scholar helped by a Government grant, he went to England and the British Museum, his object was Anglo-Saxon research. What he learned, however, of the wholesome British habit of looking upon actual life as the final test of any theory, was to prove of greater value than the translation of ancient manuscripts. And the Grundtvig schools today bear the outward and inward impress of his sojourns in England.

After a great deal of deliberation, after the publication of articles, "On Religion and Liturgy," "The Mythology of the North," and "A Short Sketch of the World's Chronicle," the composition of many poems destined to become popular hymns, and a law-suit for libel—he had charged a professor at the University with heresy—he decided to found a school. The school, or rather the school system, which he had in mind was to be like the Rugby of Thomas Arnold, an expression of Christian radicalism. It was to arouse intellectual curiosity rather than impart information. It was to appeal to the whole nation, both to the peasants and to the cultivated classes which, up to now, had been the sole patrons of poetry and science. History was to be presented as an elucidation of human life and poetry as a vitalizer of spiritual life. Such Danish Folk High Schools were to supersede in aim and method the established Latin High School—in other words, the University of Copenhagen.

Those who were to attend such a school were men and women who had finished their required education and had had some practical experience with the world. Grundtvig perceived that between the ages of eighteen and twenty there comes a great awakening when the curiosities and appetites of the mind are most alert, and the powers and desires of the soul reach out to discover and grasp the meaning of life. At this precise period adolescents should be brought into intimate contact with leaders who live with them, chat with them informally, eat with them, and discuss with them their practical problems and their personal perplexities. The pupils should be few enough and the teachers numerous and inspiring enough to make such association vital. There should be singing, some physical exercises, lectures on history, poetry, and religion, all of them applied to the spiritual enrichment of everyday life. There should be no examinations, no diplomas, and the curricula should not include technical subjects. The objective should be purely cultural, directed toward the wid-

ening of each pupil's outlook, the quickening of his aspiration, and the strengthening of his national feeling.

If we read that most of the Danes to whom Grundtvig first
unfolded his theories considered such an educational programme chimerical in the extreme, we have only to consider
how it would be received by the average hard-headed American or Englishman today. The amazing thing about Bishop
Grundtvig's conception of what a voluntary adult high school
should and could be is that there are about sixty of them functioning in Denmark today and that they are attended annually
by about ten thousand men and women from the peasant class,
from the artisan class, from the small and medium-sized farmer
class, and from ranks of tradesmen, craftsmen, and business
men. Hundreds of names in politics, business, science, and letters may be traced back to the records of one of these Folk
High Schools, and parents who attended such schools are now
sending their children to them.

Bishop Grundtvig was not a practical schoolman. (Incidentally, he was not a bishop and never held a diocese—his
title being purely honorary.) Although he conceived the idea
of such centres and laid their spiritual foundations, it was his
disciple, Christian Kold (1816–1870), who built the present
Folk High School system upon them. Kold built the Rödding
High School for one hundred and twenty-five pounds—fifty-
five of which he had saved himself and seventy of which
Grundtvig helped him collect. He acted as hod carrier during
the building, and when the thatch-roofed house was finished,
he, with his assistant and twenty-five young men pupils, slept
in the attic, using the downstairs for a schoolroom, kitchen,
and living room. Their plain living was so very plain that one
raisin apiece in the fruit soup had to suffice. But their high

thinking was high indeed. And when the day with its teaching was over, the young men and their two teachers used to discuss intellectual questions up in the darkness of the attic until they fell asleep.

Kold was a great believer in the spoken word. "When I am inspired," he said, "I can speak so that my hearers will remember what I say even beyond this world." He read aloud from Grundtvig's *Handbook of Universal History* and from those poems which are more propaganda than poetry and from the poet Ingemann's novels of medieval Denmark. While he explained that his task was to enliven the youthful mind rather than enlighten it, he insisted that his listeners give their undivided attention when he spoke. He would not even permit them to take notes lest the communion between teacher and pupil be lessened. "You may be sure that whatever you have listened to with pleasure, whatever has found really good soil in you, will certainly come up again when you have need for it."

The High School at Rödding was built (1844) in Northern Slesvig as a bulwark for Danish culture and the Danish language against German encroachment. The one in Ryslinge on the island of Fünen was built (1848–1850) to fuse the national spirit. After the defeat of 1864 all the High Schools developed into agents of regeneration, and towns grew up about them somewhat as, in the Middle Ages, towns grew up around the monasteries.

Details of curricula have changed in a hundred years, and, furthermore, each school differs somewhat from the other since it grows largely from the personality of the principal and his selected staff of teachers. Thus, the Folk High Schools at Roskilde, Esbjerg, and Möen attract pupils with socialistic tendencies; the International People's College at Elsinore stresses mutual understanding through music and manual work, whose language is international, and hopes to found a new philosophic basis for the study of our present civilization; Askov, founded by Ludvig Schröder, still seeks to perpetuate the gospel of that earnest teacher and "awake the pupils' admiration for the beauty and value of good solid practical everyday work"; Borup's High School in Copenhagen opens its lectures to the general public. Certain schools emphasize the religious life, others the handicrafts. But visits to them all, and a survey of their curricula and a comparison of their programmes, show that they are still based on the same general principles and that these principles are the original ones conceived by Grundtvig.

Although Grundtvig hoped to include all classes in his educational scheme, the majority of the pupils who attend the Folk High Schools today are from the rural districts and are between the ages of eighteen and twenty-five. In a country like Denmark everyone of that age has already received the fundamentals of education and many have attended continuation or evening school courses. While a few of these schools are coeducational (Askov takes both men and women on a one year curriculum), usually they are attended during a five or six months' winter session by young men and during a three months' summer session by young women. The schools are private institutions and are, as a rule, owned by the principal, who is also the warden. The State, however, gives them support both in a direct subsidy (graded in proportion to the salaries of the teachers, building expenses, and so forth) and in scholarships for pupils who would otherwise be unable to pay for board and tuition. This latter is about seventy to eighty

kroner a month. Such scholarships are apportioned by the
local government (the *amt*) without any stipulation as to
which High School the pupils elect. The State in no way inter-
feres with the affairs of the schools. Neither in the schools
owned by the Socialists is there socialist propaganda. In fact,
every school is supposed to be free from propaganda or proselytizing of any sort, religious or political.

The pupils and staff live together under the same roof, eat
at the same tables, and spend much time in general and in-
formal discussion. To maintain this intimacy, which is one of
the peculiar and precious features of the schools, the number
of pupils is kept to one hundred and twenty-five or less. There
are lectures—generally three during the day—which all students are expected to attend. These lectures are on history,
literature, geography, poetry, and science and do not impart
technical information but serve as an introduction to the
humanities. Thus, although the Folk High Schools are credited with having fitted the Danish people for co-operation,
there are no courses given in this subject. There are, however,
courses in sociology, and this is no longer confined to the
original restriction of discussing the Danish Constitution and
municipal administration, but includes a study of the economic situation in the world today. To be successful, co-
operation requires that all its members have a certain breadth
of vision and sufficient character not to desert the permanent
general advantage for a passing personal advantage. Such
breadth of vision and such character the Folk High Schools
endeavour to cultivate. And as an adult, voluntarily attending
lectures, can in three months acquire information which a
schoolboy reluctantly accepts in as many years, so the older
youth, having had some experience in the world, can grasp the

general principles of trust and fellowship on which co-operation depends. In the same way, there are no courses in dairying
at the Folk High Schools, and yet it is not chance that 50 per
cent of the dairy managers have attended them.

In outward form the Folk High School has changed greatly
since its inception. Teachers and pupils no longer sleep in at-
tics under thatched roofs but in modern, well-lighted, well-
heated dormitories. They gather in living rooms reminiscent
of the Oxford atmosphere which Grundtvig hoped to trans-
plant to Denmark. The class rooms and gymnasiums are not
merely adequate but compare in equipment with first-class
private schools in America or England. Although the daily
regime is simple, with early hours and plain living, it is no
longer Spartan.

It is inevitable that certain older people, remembering the
austerity of their own Folk High School days, should shake
their heads and declare that the present institutions are too
luxurious, that the lectures are either too superficial or too
dangerously radical, that Grundtvig's "wells of learning" have
been standardized into mere taps of stored information instead of being kept as living water to refresh the inner life of
youth. They point out that the Folk High School should not
be an agricultural, or a vocational, or a gymnastic, or a handicraft school—that there are plenty of these throughout the
country—but should hold ever before its eyes its mission to inspire rather than inform.

Such critics forget that "change is the pulse of life on
earth." They forget that Grundtvig, who was educated in the
Romantic Period, believed history and poetry all-important
and feared that the study of physics, chemistry, and mathematics would make students materialists as in pre-revolution-

ary France. Paul la Cour, who came later, was wiser. In the Askov High School, under the dynamic Schröder, la Cour taught mathematics and physics from the standpoint of historical development. It is not only inevitable but proper that as time has gone on there has been less talk about the Northern Gods and more talk about modern art.

It is impossible for a foreigner to weigh in the balance such criticism and its rebuttal. To him the Folk High Schools of Denmark typify a remarkable ideal and a remarkable achievement. He is more than willing to believe that they have led the youth of Denmark to liberal-mindedness, taught them to grasp the significance of events, and to take responsible positions as leaders. As long as there is progress there will be change. But the eternal verities are still supposed to be eternal. It was these verities Christian Kold had in mind when he exclaimed: "My school is the best! At Rödding they work for Danish national life as against German culture, and when the former is triumphant, the task of that school will have passed; at Hindholm they work for the rights of the peasants, and when the peasants have gained the upper hand (and they have already done so) there will be no further use for the Hindholm High School. But in my school we work for Life as against Death, and that work must continue as long as the world exists."

CHAPTER FOUR

FOREST AND HEATH

SENSITIVENESS to beauty, which Grundtvig hoped to quicken in Danish hearts, is nowhere more charmingly expressed than in their appreciation of their forests. From early spring when the first leaves cast a lozenged pattern on the carpet of white anemones below, through the summer when those same leaves spread into a canopy between earth and sky, to the autumn when the sunlight filters through them as through stained-glass windows upon their grey trunks, smooth and straight and evenly ranged or grouped as pillars in a cathedral, the beech woods are the joy of every Dane.

To go on a Sunday in summer to the great Deer Park (Dyrehaven) a few miles north of Copenhagen is a revelation not only of a beech wood forest more extensive and more beautiful than any other in Europe, but of the uses—æsthetic, scientific, and social—of such a forest. The four or five square miles of what were once the Royal Hunting Grounds stretch in grassy glades between groves of beeches, soften into moss beneath the grey trunks, extend in aisles beneath the groined arches of limbs finely moulded as carved stone. There is apparently no end to these aisles—these superb grouped clusters of trees, no

measurement of meadows blowing with wild flowers, no counting of the deer which, white and black and brown, drift across
the patches of white sunlight and dissolve into the black and
brown shadows beyond. People stroll along the roadways and
foot-paths, they stretch under the trees and sleep or read, they
spread out picnic luncheons, they pet the deer. In the winter
they toboggan, in the autumn they have paper chases. And so
vast is this lofty solitude that a hundred thousand people do
not crowd it—do not even mar its tranquillity. A hundred
thousand people are permitted to enter without charge and to
go where they wish and to do what they will—to pick wild
flowers, to nurse their babies, and court their sweethearts—
without a single prohibitory sign or a single policeman. And
not one injures a tree, frightens a deer, commits improprieties,
or leaves trash behind! Since all observe a rational code of
behaviour, all enjoy absolute freedom. An American from the
Land of Liberty is astounded by such a phenomenon.

The Deer Park is not only woods and streams and walks.
There are various amusement centres and there are cafés and
restaurants and pavilions of all descriptions. The Hermitage,
once the royal hunting lodge, is an objective for a walk or for
a drive if one will be content with a horse and carriage, for no
motor cars are permitted. There is an outdoor theatre with a
stage whose background is living trees, whose ground-cloth is
living grass, and whose wings are living shrubs and flowers.
Upon this stage, which Sir Philip Ben Greet would have delighted in, and with an audience which the New York Theatre
Guild might envy, the foreigner may see during the summer
season the classic or popular Danish plays. So excellent are the
actors—many of them from the Royal Theatre in Copenhagen
—that even a spectator who cannot understand a word can

understand the spirit of the play and follow the intention of the author. Not only Danish and German plays are given here, but Lysander has pursued Hermia through these sylvan thickets and Rosalind has found an Arden here. Realistic indeed are the effects possible in such a place. Horsemen come galloping through the woods across the very stage; torchlight processions appear dimly in the forest, approach, pass, and disappear; villains mutter and heroines flutter among the flowers; duennas peer from the cottage (or castle) window, and lovers hide in the shrubbery. In fact, when one leaves the Ulvedalene Theatre the world of illusion has so vividly materialized on actual soil before a natural forest that in some curious way the Deer Park becomes the immaterial scene. Here in the gloaming, as the light lessens, groups of people trudge down the winding roads, a man and a girl embrace under the flecked shadows of the beeches, and the half-distinguished forms and the hypnotic perspective of the setting seem more dreamlike than the figures upon the stage. In this mood we see them not as commonplace men and women but as symbols, as poets see them: as angels, leaning over the gold bar of Heaven, may view mortals far below and far away.

> "Yonder a maid and her wight
> Come whispering by:
> War's annals will cloud into night
> Ere their story die."

The Deer Park is cherished as a sanctuary where everyone can come for refreshment of body and soul. The value of such an immense free space so near the congested city is fully appreciated, as are all the forests in a country almost too compactly cultivated. But although the Danes believe "whatever is in any way beautiful . . . is complete in itself," they also believe in "the stable laws of beauty and utility." Along with the intelligent forest supervision which in the last century has doubled the wooded area in Denmark—in Jutland more than quadrupled it—so that it now occupies 9 per cent of the whole country, has gone efficient business management. In some years the Government gets from the sale of wood from Dyrehaven as much as 150,000 kroner (about $37,500). Horse-back riders who use it regularly pay a yearly fee, and the income from the amusement concessions, etc., amounts to half a million kroner (about $125,000) annually. There are plant-ings of larch, oak, birch, hawthorn, and blackthorn, and large tracts are given over to oats for the deer. There are two thousand to three thousand head of these, red and fallow. Five or six hundred have to be shot yearly—a privilege exclusive to the King and, of course, the foresters. The only elk known in Denmark is an elderly female who swam over from Sweden to North Zealand either to escape or to find a Leander.

In the Deer Park one sees in exquisite and full perfection those beeches which long ago crowded out the original forests of oak. To be sure, they have not entirely supplanted them. Wherever the oak can get light and space it still survives in huge and knotty vigour, and in those curious conflicts when a kingly oak and a queenly beech grapple together for the same throne, the oak will triumph, for his virility lasts eight hundred to a thousand years while her softer feminine span is three to four hundred. But although there are more oaks than one realizes at first glance, the impression of the Deer Park and of the typical Danish forests is of the beech, its clean, smooth, grey trunk growing straight and beautiful and—wherever there are deer to keep down the undergrowth—lending an architectural form to vistas and aisles. In Dyrehaven are plenty of deer to nibble away the small lower branches so that these particular beech wood groves are as open as great temples with ordered rows of pillars. The long free vistas are further accentuated by many grassy glades which in the old days, when the region was a royal hunting ground, were agricultural areas. Before that the Vikings buried their chieftains here. The mounds raised two thousand years ago are left undisturbed and past them flit the deer—shy, antlered shapes, pausing, quivering, vanishing into the quivering shadows.

The Deer Park is especially frequented, since it adjoins the seaside resort of Klampenborg with the smart hotels, theatres, riding school, and all the paraphernalia of fashionable vacationists. Here the holiday crowds congregate by the thousand, gay of costume and quiet of voice, like members of a country club. Even on the miles of public beaches to which bicyclists come in shoals and raise a mushroom growth of tiny bathing tents, there is no hoodlumism. In fact, the Villa Hvidöre, where the Danish-born Queen Alexandra of England and her sister, the Empress of Russia, spent many summers, is very close to this public beach. The white villa, more or less in wedding cake style, is now a hotel, and Sunday visitors drink their coffee on the terrace where once the two Queens paced. There are smart private rigs with high-stepping horses as well as old-fashioned public barouches along Strandvej. There are elegant villas as well as simple cottages between the road and the sea and certain social idealists would like to have all this land cleared of human habitation and given over to woods with vistas cut through to the ocean and free to everyone.

Although the great Deer Park is the best known and the most frequented of the Danish forests, it is not the largest of

herself to her new country. The King, debauched at seventeen, mistreated her as a bride and betrayed her as a wife. At that time the Danish Court was modelled in its elaboration and corruption upon Versailles and in its vortex was set the frightened child Queen. Within three years the King lost his health and his sanity as a result of his abnormal vices, and the physician, Struensee, who attended him was also sent to prescribe for the Queen. Eighteen years old now, Caroline Matilde lay hoping for death. Although she was the mother of the heir apparent, she was neglected by her husband, persecuted by her jealous mother-in-law, insulted by the Court which, at first delighted by her fairylike animation and amiability, soon found it expedient to ape the King's attitude. It was not strange that the unprotected girl turned more and more trustingly to the physician who was older, more tactful, more sympathetic than anyone she knew and who was her husband's confidant and adviser. Struensee, supported by both his royal patients, was made Prime Minister and became a virtual dictator. His rise to power, Caroline Matilde's passionate love for him, the plot of the Queen Mother to get control of the imbecile King and get rid of her daughter-in-law, the Masquerade Ball which was used to precipitate a Palace revolution and seize the physician and the Queen, are the exciting story which has already been discovered by novelists and moving picture writers. In the meantime, those who will take the time to read W. H. Wilkins's rather old-fashioned two volume *Queen of Tears* will not soon forget the pathetic life of Caroline Matilde, Queen of Denmark and Norway, Princess of Great Britain and Ireland, who, divorced, imprisoned, and finally given asylum in a provincial Hanoverian town, died at twenty-three. In eight years she had tasted every honour, suffered every conceivable indignity. A short span, but long enough for its unguided, unguarded possessor to reveal the frailty of a woman and the fortitude of a Queen, to display maternal love and heedless passion, to experience defeat, despair, and death. Although her name is almost forgotten in the land of her birth, her imprisonment nearly led to a war between England and Denmark. Wilkins's record of this Danish Mary Stuart gives life to an epoch, to a setting, and to a personality, all of which are romantic in the extreme.

The Castle of Frederiksborg whose royal architect, Frederik II, may have accepted suggestions from Inigo Jones, was sacked by the Swedes (1659) and several times partially destroyed by fire. In 1875 it was magnificently restored. Situated on three small islands in a lake, surmounted by towers and turrets, sumptuous in colour, ornate in design, its regality is absolute. Despite its richness and majestic bulk, it is not heavy, but as Humbert Wolfe truly observed, it suggests "a water-lily floating." This fairylike quality so infuses the tremendous mass that as the clouds move behind it, the spires seem to sway, and the wind that drives the clouds carries the sound of the chimes so that they ring far away like the bells of fairyland.

Even the interior packed with the portraits and riches of many Kings, the Knights' Hall completely lined with a hundred Gobelin tapestries and resplendent with a ceiling as intricate and rich as lapidary work, remains a castle and not a museum.

This whole section of North Zealand catches a glow from the splendour of Frederiksborg. The man in wooden shoes working in a brown field with a red-legged stork patrolling near, the mountain ash set with rosettes of scarlet berries, the white geese by a blue rivulet, the yellow fields of barley and the green ones of mangel beets—all these scenes reflect the shining romance. The whitewashed cottage walls are jewelled with fruit trees whose cherries are rubies and whose topazes are plums.

From Hilleröd to Hundested it may seem as if there were only cosy country dimpled with ponds. But just as there are forests in North Zealand, there is also heath, and what to do with the heath is more of a problem than what to do with the forests. This wiry plant whose infinitesimal flowers sweep like purple waves over miles of moorland is the delight of the artists and the despair of the farmer. The peasant cottages of turf upon these mauve and lavender uplands are picturesque, but the peasants' life upon them is heart-breaking. In 1860 a fourth of Jutland and a seventh of the whole country were heath. As early as 1788 the Government had started large wood plantations upon some of these barren moors and by 1816 had converted about thirteen hundred hectares (about three thousand two hundred and fifty acres) into fairly good spruce stands.

But it was not until 1866 that E. M. Dalgas, an officer of the Engineers, crying: "What we have lost to Germany we must make up within ourselves," founded the Danish Heath Society. The work of the Society is not confined to Jutland, though that is the region with which Dalgas's name is usually associated because there were the greatest expanses; nor is it confined to reclamation of heath land. It includes ditching, draining, and irrigating. The checking of sandflight also comes into its programme. The Danish Heath Society gives advice as to laying out plantations and arranging small shelter belts around houses and fields, and for this purpose offers plants at a low price or free. Marl is sought out and transported, for the old methods of either burning over the heath land or plough-

ing it up in furrows—first a spade and hoe were used for this
and later a trench plough—and planting evergreens and leaving
them for thirty years did not solve the entire problem. Many
rich people have laid out plantations under the supervision of
the Danish Heath Society and numbers of limited companies
have been formed with the same object. From 1885 the Government—upon the recommendation of the Society—has given
help to those who subject their plantations to Reventlow's
Forest Act of 1805. By various methods the heath of Jutland
has been reduced to half its area of 1860 and the population in
such areas has nearly doubled.

And now objections are heard that it is a mistake to convert
heath land into farm land. There is too much farming land as
it is and over-production is lowering prices for agricultural
produce. "Turn the heath into forests," says one, "Denmark
needs more woods." "Don't turn the heath into forests," says
another, "what Denmark needs more than anything else is
these free glorious open tracts," and then the well-known
adage is quoted, "Poor is the land that is solely garden."

The land certainly is not "solely garden" as one comes into
Hundested. It is all white sails of pleasure yachts and brown
nets of fishing-boats, and ferries taking their time to trundle
themselves across to Grenaa in Jutland and to Rörvig in Zealand. On the other side of the fjord—which is pronounced
without a "d" in Danish—a seaside crowd has gathered on the
beach to watch the ferry come in. White flannels and sun-back
cotton dresses proclaim it a sweltering day. It must be about
75° F. and the Danes indignantly protest that this is insuffer-
able. At any rate, it gives an excuse for the mistresses of the
attractive summer cottages at Rörvig to step out of their front

doors and stroll toward the beach as nonchalantly half-naked and brown-legged as their sisters in Nantucket or Southampton. It is not hot enough to wilt the tiny wild campanulas that grow along the roadside, and the roses that fade under a July sun in more southern latitudes last in Denmark well into August.

At Nyköbing the farming land grows richer: the road winds and—for Denmark—climbs. Of course, it does not climb steeply enough for the motorist to shift gears. But from the summit of Esterhöj—where a stone commemorates the union of South Jutland—cultivated fields on three sides and the Kattegat on the fourth comprise one of the most extended views in Zealand. The view is like many others: a pond, a tree-lined road, a windmill industriously turning, red-gold cows in green-gold fields. But it is a better view than the others, for there is more of it, and who can see too much of such a countryside? They are cutting down the shade trees along some of the roadsides and planting them along others, explaining that this is to prevent automobile accidents. There has been and still is argument about this, and it might be pointed out that although the large old trees may go and the spindly young trees may come, the telegraph poles obviously go on for ever, and a motorist can collide with one of these quite as well as with a tree if he is so inclined.

Faarevejle is marked by an irrigation canal—a part of the land reclamation project. So necessary is it for a small country like Denmark to utilize every foot of ground that the acquisition of sixteen square miles of fertile land in this region is important. In 1870 they began this particular draining and the pumps are still going. The Faarevejle Folk High School, built in 1907, on what was then an island, is now surrounded by fertile fields, and what were swamps and bogs are black-loamed gardens heavy with asparagus.

Although the dikes broke in 1920 and threw everyone into a panic, the present pumping stations and dikes look entirely efficient.

The Faarevejle Church overlooks this irrigation canal, and even if it is only a typical whitewashed church with a typical corbie-stepped gable tower and a typical red-tiled roof, on a soft summer morning it seems the prettiest one in all Denmark. Perhaps it is because it is so old—it dates from 1150—that the boxwood has had a chance to grow high about it. Perhaps it is because the masses of roses and carnations that mark the many graves flower more brightly here. Perhaps it is because of its romantic association for all English-speaking visitors. For in this distant and alien spot lies Bothwell, first the champion, then the lover, and finally the husband of Mary, Queen of Scots.

A strip of drugget is rolled back from the floor of the church. A trap-door is unlocked and lifted and a ladder placed in position. In the cramped crypt—which is only a bit of cellar—lying in his coffin and revealed by a glass panel—may be seen the man who had the villainy first to superintend the blowing up of Kirk o' Field where Darnley lay and then the audacity to declare it "the strangest accident that ever chancit, to wit, the fouder [lightning] came out of the luft [sky] and had burnt the king's house." Time has shredded away clothes and flesh and yet has left the face perfectly preserved. All flesh is clay indeed, even the flesh of this "glorious, rash, and hazardous young man." Wicked he undoubtedly was, "as naughty a man as liveth and much given to the most detestable vices," wrote Cecil's correspondents. But proud he was also and the final humiliation must be the denial of privacy even in death.

Going out into the open air we reflect that the fourth Earl of Bothwell, Duke of Orkney and Shetland, might have chosen a grander but hardly a sweeter spot, and begin to recall just how he came to be buried here at all. After the murder of Darnley, he married Darnley's wife and was ultimately driven from England. He fled to Norway, was dismissed from that country by the authorities, and arrived in Copenhagen, where he blandished King Frederik II from surrendering him by promising to restore to Denmark the Orkneys and Shetland. He was removed to Sweden and after Mary's downfall—he had been forced to submit to a divorce from her on pleas that recall those of Henry VIII and Catherine of Aragon—his good treatment came to an end. He was sentenced to solitary confinement in the Castle of Dragsholm in Zealand, Denmark—a fearful punishment for a full-blooded warrior.

To Dragsholm Castle then we betake ourselves, past red clover fields and a co-operative dairy on the main road, past the farm buildings on a private road, under a lordly gate into a cobbled courtyard with three sides enclosed by the flat white façades of the Castle and the fourth by a crenellated wall. An enormous, empty, echoing barracks of a place, with eighty rooms and a private chapel in white and blue. It is for sale, cheap, and although it is six hundred years old, it has not only been kept in repair but modernized. There is a bathroom in it! Here, below the level of daylight, in what was later used as a wine cellar, the man whom Mary, Queen of Scots, had loved so ardently was imprisoned for the last five years of his life. So perhaps even the church cellar with its occasional visitors may seem acceptably sociable after those days and nights which ended in insanity.

Forests, heath, drained land—one can study these various departments of Denmark's land reclamation programme in North Zealand although, as a matter of fact, there are more forests and much more heath in Middle Jutland. Eighty years ago North Jutland began to check sandflight by planting the dunes with marram grass, heather, and mountain pine.

To Jutland we must go, but return to Copenhagen first, as one always seems to be doing in Denmark.

And so back past Asnaes with its factory for threshing machines, past a co-operative general store, past a dike and a pumping station, past Holbaek and the plant school at Vipperöd. The sound of a village blacksmith rings through the late afternoon quiet. Coffee is being served under the trees of a wayside inn. And so, past the spires of Roskilde and into Copenhagen and to the end of the round tour of the island of Zealand.

PART III

Beyond the Borders

CHAPTER ONE

CHIMNEYS, CRANES, AND QUARRIES

T HE farmer fills—and rightly—such an important place in the economic and political life of Denmark, and the farms and cultivated fields extend in such conspicuous beauty over the Danish landscape, that the average visitor is surprised to learn that while thirty per cent of the population is engaged in agriculture, the same per cent is engaged in industry.

Such surprise is comprehensible, for although the industrial production is practically equal to the agricultural, Denmark has none of those grime-laden factory cities with their squalid outskirts such as blacken the face and fame of America and England.

An over-night boat from Copenhagen—not only as clean as a whistle but in its miniature fashion quite as complete and elegant as a transatlantic liner—arrives at Aalborg in North Jutland in the fresh morning air, and the ribbons of white smoke, the distant sound of a whistle, and the glitter of the lime cliffs announce that it is one of the important manufacturing centres of the country.

It would be possible to spend an agreeable week in Aalborg

and hardly be conscious of its factories, for the gay modernity of the hotels and cafés of the twentieth-century city and the handsome antiquity of the eleventh-century town offer entertainment for every taste. Here are not only the twisting by-streets and Mother Goose cottages with rumpled red roofs that make all Denmark seem like a picture-book, but the Castle of Christian III, the Gothic House of King Hans—both of them from the sixteenth century—and the superb stone mansion which Jens Bang built in 1624 with high-pitched gables and elaborate façade, which prove that for four hundred years this Jutland city has been the home of wealth and tradition.

The streets are full of life, and the bridge which spans the Limfjord is crowded, for Aalborg is the centre of all this region for business men and pleasure seekers. Indeed, so animated is the centre of the city that the factory districts, a mile further out, seem quiet in comparison.

In fact, the quietness of the largest Portland Cement Works in Scandinavia is astonishing. The most tremendous revolving kiln in the world—it is eighteen feet in diameter—never stops. The tallest smoke-stack in Northern Europe is never cold. Four or five hundred workmen are busy here day and night packing every twenty-four hours one hundred and forty thousand bags of cement which are shipped from the company's own harbour to countries all over the globe. This highly specialized activity is set in the midst of fields. Its raw material lies in the back yard, and water for easy transportation of its finished product—and for the coal brought for fuel from England and Poland—lies in the front yard. Lime is Denmark's only mineral resource and she makes the most of it. She has cement factories from Aalborg to Tönder. They make tiles and pipes and cement blocks for building and not only is cement found on the lists of major exports but cement-making machinery has a widely extended foreign market.

Another great industry which also uses native raw material is the Danske Spritfabrikker which manufactures spirit and yeast and has in Aalborg, and in Hobro a few miles south, distilleries remarkable for their size, their management, and their history.

Denmark has no prohibition problem, and the temperance question has been settled so permanently and satisfactorily that there is little interest in the subject. As a matter of fact, there has never been much agitation about it. No prohibition bill has ever come before Parliament. This does not mean that there was never any drunkenness. Until 1916 Denmark had the reputation—and the statistics proved that it was, unfortunately, well deserved—of being the hardest drinking nation in the world. The rate of consumption of spirits is now almost the lowest in all Europe, so low that doctors have difficulty finding delirium tremens cases as specimens for their medical students. In the course of forty years (1871–1911) the consumption of spirits dropped practically one-half. From 1906 to 1920 it dropped to one-eighth of its previous figure. And this amazing record was not due to any legal prohibitionary measures but entirely to voluntary action. The "voluntary" action was, of course, prepared for and encouraged by education, by improved social conditions, and, most of all, by an excessive taxation on spirits. And although the workman may recall with regret the days when the bottle of *akvavit* (which at present costs 8.85 kroner) cost about 55 öre (before 1912), the Danes as a whole have accepted the present conditions philosophically. There is no restriction on the amount one can buy except his ability to pay for it, and liquor shops keep the same hours as other shops. Smuggling is handled by a treaty agreement with other countries, all shipments of liquor coming in or going out being supervised and announced in advance. Bootlegging is controlled by all bottles being closed with an official seal and to counterfeit this is as grave an offence as to counterfeit money. Of course there is still occasional smuggling. There are still total abstainers, local option and temperance societies, and a stranger who sees "Alcohol er Gift" in large letters over a public house need not proceed on the assumption that there are free drinks within. In such a hostelry there are no drinks at all, free or otherwise, for "gift" is "poison" in Danish, and although the accuracy of such a statement may be questioned, the fact remains that there are still people, even in Denmark, who believe it to be the dismal truth.

There is no better index to the whole subject than the Danske Spritfabrikker in Aalborg. At the commencement of the nineteenth century there were about twenty-five hundred lawful distilleries in the country. In 1914 there were about twenty-five. Today there is one. This concentration started more than a hundred years ago, but it was fulfilled during the War. Then the small distilleries found themselves in difficulties because of high taxation. Thereupon two of the largest concerns got the right to buy out all other existing plants, to abandon them or include them, provided the personnel of such plants was remunerated. The State kept a certain control (such as the limitation of the quantity of distillation).

When the two concerns were merged into one a new arrangement was made (1923) between it and the State, which places the former in a sort of leasehold to the latter. There is no State liquor monopoly in Denmark as in many other countries, but the Danske Spritfabrikker has a concession (until 1944) for producing, selling, and exporting yeast, *akvavit,* and alcohol. Its distilleries, yeast factories, refrigerated railway carriages, the experimental potato farms from which some of its raw material is obtained—the rest of the potatoes and barley are bought from farmers in the open market—are all of the highest type. Although only ten per cent of the produce is for drinking—the rest is for commercial purposes, explosives, varnishes, denatured alcohol, and so forth—to that ten per cent one owes the thimbleful of *akvavit* which, with smoked herring or other savoury titbits, is the fiery precursor of every proper Danish meal, and the excellent liqueurs which are its finale. The yeast production is sufficient for all the many varieties of Danish bread—each one better than the other—and also has a large foreign market.

The Cement Works and the Distillery both use not merely native but local material, so it is obvious why Aalborg should have been chosen for their factories. But there are other industries dependent upon imported raw material, and upon one of these—Obel's Tobacco Factory—a great part of the population of the city depends, directly or indirectly, for its living. The tobacco comes from America, Turkey, and Greece, and one-half the price of the finished product goes into duty. Nevertheless, in this country where even the ladies smoke cigars—the rather small, light ones, it should be added—and the cigarette is ubiquitous, and snuff has its devotees, the prices are not excessive. In an industry where, despite all modern machinery, the human hand remains the chief implement, fifteen hundred employees—mostly women—work in eight-hour shifts and one generation of Carmens follows another into the factory with remarkable cheerfulness. Not that such sequence is inevitable.

Here, as all over Denmark, there is opportunity for anyone of ability to rise, the particular case in this connexion being Prime Minister Stauning—a statesman of exceptional astuteness and holding his office for eight consecutive years, which is unprecedented—who was at one time a cigar sorter.

The edible oils industry is another example of a highly successful manufacture dependent upon imported raw material. Edible oils are indispensable to a country where margarine is used by most of the people and cattle cake used by all of the farmers. Five hundred thousand tons of soy beans, palm oil, cottonseed oil, and so forth must be imported yearly to supply this demand, and yet the factories find it profitable to manufacture not only a sufficient amount for home consumption but for export as well. At present the manufacture is maintained on such a scale that one-third of Denmark's industrial export consists of edible oils. The same situation is repeated in the manufacture of printer's ink and also of varnishes—the raw material for the latter coming from thirteen different countries and five continents and being exported to more than forty countries.

The Federation of Danish Industries emphasizes that one-fourth of all Danish export is industrial and believes that Danish economic life will be more prosperous and the balance of trade more stable if she continues to develop along industrial lines instead of concentrating exclusively upon agriculture—which brings us back to the perennial conflict between the agricultural and industrial parties.

Neither are the industrialists solidly united, for there are free factories and shops and there are also co-operative ones. Yet the co-operative movement in Denmark differs somewhat from that in other Scandinavian countries in that it has been more definitely specialized as regards agriculture. To be sure, there are co-operative building societies and co-operative banks and even co-operative sanatoria, but a system of Government loans has more or less reduced the necessity for these organizations. And, to be sure, the co-operatives have their great flour mills and margarine factories and manufacture shoes and soap and clothes—practically all the necessities. But the movement was originally based upon the needs of the farming class, and the co-operative shops are still chiefly evident in the rural districts. In these districts their turnover approximates that of the free shops. The co-operative shops started with groceries, dried fish, rice, and margarine—what is called colonial produce—and gradually extended to hardware, farming implements, and clothing, so that today a co-operative shop in the country is very much like an old-fashioned "country store."

All Scandinavia has been familiar with the co-operative principle for so many years and has found it so practical for its needs and congenial to its temperament that any Scandinavian knows exactly how to go about organizing, financing, and maintaining a local co-operative society and how to connect that local society with a Central Co-operative. A Co-operative raises its own capital and out of the net proceeds interest is paid on that capital at a fixed rate. (Herein lies one of its differences from a stock company where the entire net proceeds are divided among the shareholders.) The rest of the net proceeds of a co-operative society goes to the members according to their purchases—in dairies according to the milk they deliver.

The principle of co-operation—agricultural and industrial, in regard to purchase and production, import and export—

seems entirely simple to the Danish mind. But this does not mean that all Danes believe in either its theory or its practice. For while the co-operative shops all insist that they introduce and maintain wholesome competition, that they have successfully fought cartels and trusts and forced prices down to the advantage of the consumer, the free shops sing a different tune. They, too, are organized (with a membership of ten thousand merchants from outside of Copenhagen) in order to put through certain laws. They believe that the Co-operative Central is too large and destroys initiative, that it is better to let the individual operate freely. They emphasize the injustice of the co-operative shops paying no taxes on their manufacturing plants or their shops and, therefore, having an unfair advantage over the free shops. They point out that in the old days the nobles were the privileged ones and allowed to go tax-free. Today the same abuse of privilege is repeated with the co-operative shops and it is as unfair now as it was then.

And while the industrialists and the agriculturists engage in arguments which sharpen the wits of both, and while the co-operative shops and the free shops wrestle for advantage, the trade union has, since the beginning of the seventies, penetrated every nook and cranny of them all. The eight-hour day, the prohibition of child labour—a boy may be apprenticed at fourteen under a foreman for four years, but eighteen is the legal age for regular employment—the care of the union for its unemployed members and the insistence that such members be engaged when there is a vacancy—all these familiar features are repeated in Denmark as in America and England. As in other small northern countries with a homogeneous and well-educated population, the conditions for the workers are uniformly admirable. One has merely to walk through any factory and look at the employees to see how well fed, well dressed, and well conditioned they are. Steam baths, showers, locker rooms, dining-rooms where they can bring their own luncheons or buy what they want at a low price—these are practically universal features. To be sure, there are strikes by workmen dissatisfied with wages and there is irritation on the part of the employers when they are forced to hire incompetents because the union insists upon it. But a survey of the wage lists and a visit to practically any sort of workshop, manufacturing plant, or factory, supplemented by one to the quarters in which the workers live, reveals a social standard extremely and consistently high.

The industrialist party and the agriculturist party argue and the free shops and the co-operative shops engage in wholesome competition and the trade unions keep busy with them all. But there is one prosperous class of workers who refuse to trouble their heads unduly about such matters. The twenty thousand fishermen who skirt the coast and who plough the deep sea as far as Iceland are neither employers nor employees but independent men following the immemorial tradition of their ancestors.

There is no place where one can better see a fishing fleet than near Skagen, and no better way to get to Skagen than from Aalborg, across the Limfjord—famous for its oysters—and along the road through Hjallerup, which used to be the largest horse market in Europe, as many as ten thousand horses being sold during the annual June fair. Now only a paltry five thousand change hands during the three days. Frederikshavn has shipbuilding yards and it has also a tree-shaded promenade along the coast and a good harbour which ships are glad enough to slip into when the weather keeps them from doubling the Skaw.

And now the country begins to flatten out—if that were possible—and in the distance one sees, as on a coloured map, Skagen, that northernmost tip of Jutland where the Kattegat and the Skagerrak meet in spray and turmoil. This is the region of yellow broom and purple heather, the scene of drying brown fish nets draped like giant cobwebs, of humble fisher cottages, of vacation camps, sand dunes, and scrub pines. Old Skagen has become a summer colony with horseback riders and wicker bath chairs and beach hotels and brightly dressed bathers, and artists setting up their easels amid the sand dunes, and literary pilgrims inquiring the way to the cairn-like tomb of the poet Holger Drachmann and to his home, Villa Pax.

However, Skagen still remains a fishing village—the largest fishing village in Denmark—and the harbour is full of motor boats, row-boats and sail boats, and the air is full of the smell of fresh fish, wet sails, and dripping seines. Down by the water front stands the auctioneer, surrounded by a dozen buyers, with tally boards slung from around their necks. The auctioneer knows his business. He knows the current price for the iridescent mackerel, for the still slapping flounder, for the eight hundred pound tunny, for the haddock being scooped alive from the storage wells in the bottom of the boats. The buyers know their business, too, and by a nod or a wink so slight as to be imperceptible to any but the auctioneer, they make their bids and drive their bargains.

The fishermen are making fast their boats, their sons lending a hand, novitiates in that order to which they are already destined to belong. In the trim cottages yonder the fishermen's wives are boiling fresh cod-fish and new potatoes and making a mustard sauce to complete a meal worth travelling to Skagen to eat. The fishermen's daughters are at work in the summer hotels, or in the factory close by where there is great bustle of smoking and canning and shipping. Fifty thousand boxes of sardines and fifteen thousand boxes of prawns are only two items in the day's output; the mackerel in olive oil is bound for the Catholic countries of middle Europe, the waste will be made into fertilizer.

There is no union labour in the factory at Skagen and unionism does not flourish among the fishermen. Each man owns his own boat, or a syndicate of three to five owns a boat together. There are only a few shipping companies with paid crews. For the Skagen fisherman is not a "joiner." He may be a member of a local fisherman's association and often of a co-operative fish marketing association for the disposal of his catch in Denmark and abroad, and he must, whether he will or no, be a member of the Insurance Association of Danish Fishermen and Sailors. To command a sea-going vessel, he must have passed an examination in navigation at a school authorized by the Government. But in outlook and in managing his affairs he is an individualist and when he accepts a loan from the Government for a new boat or a new seine it is with the air of a business man negotiating a business deal.

The Government does well to assist its fishermen with loans and its fisheries with an annual subsidy (through the Danish Fishermen's Association). It does well to support fishing schools and signal stations and grants for research work and to supervise these things under the Fisheries Directorate. For the trade which yields between three and four million dollars annually gives direct employment to about twenty thousand men—and indirectly to hundreds of net makers, boat builders, and so forth—and provides the Danish table with a hundred delicious dishes.

It is a stern trade, however, that of a Skagen fisherman. One realizes it, looking at their faces tanned by the salt spray and the wind. One realizes it, walking through the graveyard where, among the few British Marines and the Germans who lost their lives in the Battle of Jutland and were washed ashore in May 1916, stand the many memorial stones to the seamen who have perished in the North Sea. It is a strange wild place, this Northern Jutland, and one realizes this, too, standing by that church which was buried by a sand-storm in the eighteenth century and whose tower only is visible.

Aalborg, well toward the north of Jutland, and Fredericia, well toward the south, are posts between which hang a chain of towns nearly every one of which may be delighted in for its well-preserved ancient buildings, splendid and simple, or may be regarded as links in the chain of industries. Thus, Mariager has large cement works, and Randers, with its sign of the salmon like Boston's sign of the cod, has the great yeast factory of the Spritfabrikker and the carriage works which supply the rolling stock of the State Railway. The country-side between Aalborg and Fredericia—this, too, may be looked at like more fluttering pages in that picture-book of green fields, blue ponds, and white cottages which is Denmark, or it may be appraised from a utilitarian angle. Thus, the billowing potato fields—as innocent of bugs as primal Eden was of serpents—are laboratories producing raw material for spirits, and the black-and-white cattle—for the Holstein breed is here—are auxiliaries of the condensed milk factories.

In the midst of the crowding roofs, masts mark the canals.

ALLEGHENY COLLEGE LIBRARY

In this fairylike metropolis twisted dragon tails seem quite a proper finish for the Bourse.

ALLEGHENY COLLEGE LIBRARY

The Lur Blowers Column. The lur—a primitive trumpet distinctive of Denmark—is still carried in national festivals.

ALLEGHENY COLLEGE LIBRARY

Fish-sellers' stands in the open.

ALLEGHENY COLLEGE LIBRARY

Aarhus, however, cannot be slid past with such brief mention, for it is not only the capital of Jutland but the second largest and second oldest city in Denmark, with a cathedral dating from the thirteenth century, and a Dominican monastery which is now used as an Old People's Home, and with venerable houses doubled in number by their reflection in a canal-like river. Here are ambitious factories. Here is the new University—the only one besides the University at Copenhagen and the country's best example of modern architecture —and here is, if not the oldest, certainly its most fascinating, medieval city.

It is not a genuine city, although every stick and stone in it is genuine. "The Old Town" of Aarhus is apparently occupied and functioning, with its mill by the side of the stream and with jars of fresh peppermint candy in the apothecary shop. Down its narrow streets, shaded by a half-timbered overhang and by a suspended gallery, past its fountain in the open market-place, people stroll or stand to look about them. The shops and offices, the dining-rooms and kitchens, the drawing-rooms and bedchambers are rarely without occupants. Yet all these buildings of yellow and white, salmon, tomato, and ochre that settle so cosily to the ground, all these solid beams of black and brown and terra-cotta are importations to Aarhus. So are the chairs and tables and pictures and dishes and costumes. Buildings and furnishings alike were threatened by that march of progress which is no respecter of age. They were saved from demolition, bought, taken down, brought to the park here, and set up by skilful hands exactly as they had originally been. The town seems complete with its Mayor's House, workshops, dwellings, and mill. It is waiting, however, for a typical church to be threatened by a railroad or a factory.

When this final memento of an architectural age that is past has been rescued from destruction and set up in Aarhus for a renewed and honoured cycle of existence, "The Old Town" will be complete.

Aarhus is delightful. One could spend a week or a month there with never a dull moment. In "The Old Town," in the city proper, in the University, antiquarians, architects, historians, and plain or garden variety tourists will be instructed without pain and without price and entertained into the bargain. The collector will discover treasures everywhere and discover, too, that the Danes know the value of antiques quite as well as he does.

But the pages of the picture-book are only a quarter turned, the text is only a quarter read.

The visitor to Denmark must find his way to Mindeparken, that vast outdoor circus with a rose garden above it and a King's Castle beyond it and patterns on its chalk stone walls made by the names of four thousand volunteers who died in the Great War—a tremendous roster for a country the size of Denmark. The chalk stone is from France where they fell and the simplicity of the design—nothing but a circular theatre with four bas-reliefs and four thousand names engraved upon the walls—is an impressive war memorial.

South of Marselisborg is Horsens with its harbour and its shipping. South of Horsens is Vejle on its tree-clad fjord. North-west of Vejle is Jellinge, with its two tumuli and its famous tenth-century rune stone on which Harald Bluetooth commemorates his father Gorm, "the King who won all Denmark and Norway and Christianized the Danes."

And south of Vejle is Fredericia. This busy terminus is visited not so often because of the Castle built by Frederik III, or the ramparts which are now promenades, or for Bissen's statue of the Brave Foot-Soldier, commemorating the Second Slesvig War, but because of its important industrial exhibition. Once a year for a fortnight it opens its pavilions and booths: it has banquets and speeches, it collects and displays a graphic survey of Denmark's industrial progress. Porcelains and paintings as well as electrical contrivances and machinery, linens and fabrics as well as fish and cheese, furniture as well as margarine, and motors as well as leather goods. The exhibition at Fredericia shows how Denmark—one of the poorest countries in Europe in raw material—is manufacturing goods sufficient for nearly all her home consumption and for a generous export. It is the best argument that industrialists could offer as to why they do not want to import finished goods from Germany; it is their best proof that industrial life, engaging over one-third of the population of the country, is as essential as agriculture to national prosperity.

CHAPTER TWO

FRIENDLY FLAGS

IT may surprise many Americans to know that on every
Fourth of July when the length and breadth of the United
States is billowing with flags and resounding with patriotic
speeches and, alas, frequently being deluged with thunder
showers, the same flags, the same speeches, and too often the
same rain are equally omnipresent in Denmark. Not all over
Denmark, to be sure, but in a certain tract of four hundred
acres in Jutland which, since 1911, has been dedicated to this
special purpose.

Rebild National Park is the only place outside America
where America's Independence Day is regularly celebrated.
It is the only park on the globe established specifically for
Fourth of July celebrations. It is unique among international
monuments to peace.

Although Rebild is always open to the public and one
hundred thousand people visit it in course of the year, on
the Fourth of July the rolling heath land displays on every
little hill-top an American and a Danish flag and from the
entrance gate to the speakers' stand sets up a double row of
poles bearing the flags of the different states of the Union,

many of which the visiting American must admit are quite
unfamiliar to him. To this remote spot come trekking on this
day from thirty to forty thousand people, each one paying a
krone to get into the grounds, many of them bringing picnic
luncheons and every last one of them standing up on the rough
incline of the hills or sitting on the prickly heath for the two
or three hours of the speech making, even if the rain comes
down in torrents, as, for some as yet unascertainable reason, it
usually seems to do for this particular celebration either in the
United States or Denmark.

Who are these thirty or forty thousand people? Why do they
come to Rebild? How long have they been coming? And who
started such an idea in a country so far removed, geographically and economically, from the United States?

In 1905 Ivar Kirkegaard, who was the editor of a Danish
language magazine published in Racine, Wisconsin, called a
meeting of Danish-born Americans for the purpose of promot-
ing closer cultural relations between the Danish immigrants
in America and their kinspeople in the mother country. An
annual reunion in Denmark was to be part of this alliance.
In 1906 the Danish-American Association was formed with
Henry L. Hertz of Chicago as president, and in 1911, under
the direction of Dr. Max Henius, also of Chicago, over a thousand Danish-born Americans and many thousands of Danes
gathered at an exposition in Aarhus in honour of the first
Fourth of July celebration on Danish soil.

The purchase of two hundred acres—subsequently raised
to four hundred acres—of moorland, the presentation of its
deed to King Christian X as a gift of Danish-born Americans
to their mother country, the forming of the Danish Rebild
Committee and the Rebild National Park Board followed. A

special arrangement placed the Park under American control with the Danish Ministry of Agriculture in charge of supervision and maintenance. Except for the interruption of the World War, the Fourth of July has been celebrated here annually since 1912, filling the front pages of the Danish newspapers and being broadcast to the United States. Not far from the speakers' platform a Lincoln log cabin—the wood, windows, even the hardware shipped from America—serves as an emigrant museum, with a covered wagon, Indian costumes, and various objects associated with the early Danish-American pioneers.

In the Emigrant Archives Building—an old manor-house outside of Aarhus—more serious students will find every conceivable kind of data: letters, diaries, autobiographies, eight thousand bound volumes and many thousands of unbound ones, manuscripts, pamphlets, and brochures connected with Danish emigrants in the United States, Canada, Australia, South America, New Zealand, and South Africa. Here are files of newspapers published for and by Danish emigrants all over the world. Here is a Rare Book Room, donated by Dr. Max Henius, old prints, everything connected with those Danes who have left Denmark and who with their descendants number in the United States alone over half a million.

As a reminder of the earliest emigrants of all, not far from the Lincoln log cabin is a nine-ton boulder brought down from near Oslo by a glacier some twelve thousand years ago. In 1933 it was placed on the hill where it now stands and the runic characters at its base explain: "The Cimbri went forth from these parts in 120 B.C."

Unlike a political issue where the conclusion of the majority is apt to be less intelligent than that of its individual members, an idealistic project may soar higher than a single aspiration. The Fourth of July celebration at Rebild is genuinely impressive, and in a world whose members are more given to dissenting than assenting, such friendly alliance between two nations merits respect.

Danish emigrants are such a valuable ethnic contribution to the land of their adoption that the United States may well regret that under the present quota regulations only four or five hundred are annually permitted to enter. One such emigrant boy "came near to being the ideal American citizen," according to no less an authority than Theodore Roosevelt. Jacob Riis, who managed to love and honour both the United States and Denmark, was born in Jutland, further south, in Ribe, and the house of his birth bears a plaque commemorating its famous son. Even without Jacob Riis, Ribe would attract Americans, for it is not only the oldest town in Denmark and one of the most picturesque, but in the open square outside the Cathedral a medieval morality play is given, every three years, to an attentive and even reverent audience.

The trip to Ribe from whatever direction it is made, passes through country wilder, more open than that of Zealand, with the isolated farmhouse group set back further in its mauve and lavender and tawny fields. Viewed through this longer perspective it gains a different air—characteristic of Jutland and of no other part of Denmark.

The road passes oak trees, very old and very gnarled, and tremendous farms whose tarred beams are as hard and black as iron. In the garden of one of these great homesteads of Tjele, among roses and honeysuckle, Marie Grubbe flitted through her white and golden girlhood. And in that same garden, given over to vegetables and permeated with harshness and greed, passed those years when "whatever had been delicate and flowerlike in her nature, all the fair and fragrant growth which heretofore had entwined her life as with luxurious though fantastic and even bizarre arabesques, withered and died the death. Coarseness in thought as in speech, a low and slavish doubt of everything great and noble, and a shameless self-scorn were the effect of these sixteen years at Tjele."

To recreate the lovely unfolding and the sordid close of that spirit took Jens P. Jacobsen four years—not long for the making of what Georg Brandes called one of the greatest *tours de force* in Danish literature, but long for an artist who knew he must die at forty. Whoever would follow the monotony of existence as it was nearly three hundred years ago on a great farm in Jutland—the making of candles, the mixing of mead, the milking, the haying—has only to open the pages of *Marie Grubbe*. And whoever would follow the unconscious steps by which a maid in lavender homespun and billowing linen ruffles blooms in a madder-red robe and clocked stockings into the bride of an aristocrat, coarsens into a slovenly, sensual farmwife, and then finally degenerates into a pair of arms wielding the oars of the Falster ferry, may open these same pages. The great house at Tjele still stands, half concealed by trees, and so does the ferryman's cottage, low to the dust of the road on the island of Falster and, among the seductive women whose outward history is actually known and whose inward history may thereby be surmised, Jacobsen has placed for all time the portrait of this seventeenth-century gentlewoman. "As a fair and noble edifice in the hands of barbarians is laid waste and spoiled, the bold spires made into squat cupolas, the delicate, lace-like ornaments broken bit by bit, and the wealth of pictures hidden under layer upon layer of deadening whitewash, so was Marie Grubbe laid waste and spoiled in those sixteen years."

South of Tjele lies Viborg, one time the capital of Jutland and now its county seat, with a royal residence and an eleventh-century cathedral whose walls have been decorated by Joakim Skovgaard, with frescoes remarkable for their heroic size, their vigour, and their piety. Hald Castle is not far away, nor, as the motor flies, are the Silkeborg Lakes with their Paradise Islands and Heaven's Mountain—Himmelbjerget—and all the little ferry boats and yachts and piers and landing stages.

At Baekkelund the soil, which in Zealand and North Jutland is as free from stones as Ireland is from snakes, confesses to an occasional rock. There are even a few field stone buildings and stone walls. At Knudstrup the road skirts an inn where the landlord is smoking a meerschaum pipe with a dachshund at his feet and where in the morning sunshine a group of strawberry merchants are just dispersing from their dance of the night before.

It pushes on through sandier soil; past peat bogs and stretches of heath ploughed in furrows and planted with evergreens; climbs high across moors and uplands—more primitive, more extended than the cultivated fields of Zealand, with even a breath of pioneer life in the air of the rolling hills. In the fields graze sheep, quite properly separated from the goats which are tethered more humbly by the roadside.

It leads into Herning, the centre of those small towns described in *Knitting Room Tales* from which ambitious lads like American newsboys with a bundle of papers used to start out to make their way in the world, only the Jutland youths carried parcels of knitted goods on their backs. Here in the

provincial hotel one sees the picture and hears again the name
of Dalgas who started the reclamation of the heath. Near To-
böl the first stork looks down from an untidy nest on a ridge-
pole.

And now, floating above that flat plain which stretches from
the North Sea to an estuary of the Rhine, rise the two spires—
one pointed and one square—of Ribe Cathedral, the oldest in
Denmark and possibly in all Scandinavia.

Ribe has the pretty air of complacency of a place which has
always been loved, and accepts as a right in its old age the
same flattery it did not question in its youth. And it is a darling place, with its narrow streets lined by buildings whose
doors and windows all sag a little and whose walls are a trifle
out of plumb and whose tiled roofs are a jumble of angles.
Inside the houses are walls panelled, frescoed, or lined with
tiles, blue-and-white and brown-and-white. Iron-bound chests
stand in the narrow passageways, plants bloom on every casement sill, the brass knockers and door knobs are polished pro-
digiously.

The oldest cathedral in Denmark has been so vigorously
restored that it looks like the newest. Originally built of vol-
canic stone brought from the shores of the Rhine over the
North Sea to this rockless village, the edifice has been reno-
vated with identical material. The result is as successful as if a
lady of sixty had had her face lifted and could pass for a girl of
sixteen. But this disconcertingly fresh surface softens as the
daylight softens and the good proportions of the Cathedral
come into their own.

The stone façade makes an excellent sounding-board for the
outdoor play, and the large square offers accommodation for
the hundreds of spectators. The first play was given in 1936

and up a stairway built against the Lutheran Cathedral, Every-
man ascended to a Roman Catholic Paradise and descended
down it into a Roman Catholic Purgatory. Faith, in blue and
silver, held a Cross before his eyes; Good Deeds, in white, accompanied him; and the Devil, in hoofs and claws, gnashed
his teeth in disappointment. The light streamed through the
leaded windows, the clang of the bell and the swell of the organ
mingled, and only the storks, as they braked their speed in the
air and settled down on their nests on the neighbouring ridge-
poles, reminded the motionless audience that this morality
play, universal in the Christian world for more than eight
Christian centuries and poignantly comprehensible in whatever tongue it is given, was unfolding its lesson in Ribe in
Denmark.

There are other sounds in Ribe than the organ and the bell.
During the summer a night watchman with a lighted lantern
walks the streets waking people up with his reassuring chant
that it is safe for them to go to sleep. There is the perpetual
intermittent whir of storks who flap the long miles to South
Africa every fall and the long miles back to Ribe every spring,
as safe in Denmark as the albatross upon the sea, symbols of
peace to the house they choose to nest upon, and busy here,
as elsewhere, bringing babies to waiting mammas, although in
Ribe a child is more likely to get a little brother or sister if
he scatters some sugar on the window sill. The stork apparently is ready for something sweet after a diet of marsh frogs
and lizards.

And there is the sound of the factory—a radiator factory, of
all things!—and of the plant for assembling and repairing motor cars, and the soft whiz of bicycles as the workers go to and
fro, and of wooden shoes as the labourers clatter on the pave-

ment. For Ribe, despite its age, is still active and industrious. And there is the sound of thunder which, in dog days, comes and goes with the tides.

A little outside the town there is another sound—the wind clattering reeds of what was a moat of King Valdemar's Castle. The Ribehus is gone and the hill is marked by a statue of Queen Dagmar, whose name even after seven centuries still seems to have power to charm the Danish ear. Many legends have gathered about this Bohemian Princess of whom we know little except that she was loving and beloved and that she died in her husband's absence. Hearing the news, he came galloping so furiously that he left all his courtiers far behind and his grief and her love so prevailed that she was permitted to come back from Purgatory to bid him good-bye.

> *"She went up slowly to the gate,*
> *And then, just as of yore,*
> *She turn'd back at the last to wait*
> *And say farewell once more."*

Besides all these sounds there are the sights—the many "gossip mirrors" prove it—admirable devices fastened in front of a window, not only reflecting the street in both directions but bringing the far-off things near and intensifying those which are at hand, thereby achieving in their simple confines the philosophy of the poet and the aspiration of the painter.

Yes, all sorts of things happen in Ribe, and perhaps the familiar ones are best, as when the loads of hay come slowly down the long straight road across the plains, or a little boat slips up the shallow stream which was once a deep waterway bearing ships laden with wine from the Rhine and silk and cloth from Flemish towns. Now the river is a shallow thread, content to meander through the meadows and turn the wheels of the flour mill.

From the top of the Cathedral tower one can look out over the interminable marsh land spreading in every direction with the bright rim of water beyond it. Over this great plain in the spring many times that water has crept and crawled toward Ribe; has risen and reared so that in 1634 it stood five feet above the floor of the Cathedral which is on the highest land in the town. Even as late as 1909 and 1911 the meadows have been swirling waves whose height is indicated on a handsome memorial column in the town. Now there are dikes along the coast, but many a Prayer Book falls open to the words: "Preserve, O Lord, the dikes and dams in the King's Marsh Lands: watch over the widows and the fatherless."

The plain and the sea are as much a part of Ribe as the streets and the cloistered medieval monastery and Church of St. Catherine, now used as a home for old ladies, and the sound of thunder is as much a part of Ribe as the sound of the Cathedral bell. Jacob Riis in *The Old Town* tells it all with veracity and love, and whoever would recall Ribe or whoever anticipates a visit there could not do better than to turn to his volume. For in it is not only the history and folk lore of his birthplace but the childhood of "the staunchest, most efficient friend the children of New York City ever had." A mist of feeling floats over the pages of *The Old Town* like the mist which rises from its marshes, becoming at night white wraiths walking over the land between the town and the water. "The same storm, having gone out to sea with the ebb, would come back on the flood tide and keep the farmers awake who lived under a roof of thatch. Good cause: I have seen as many as half a score of farmhouses burning after a long night's storm.

Thus, too, people died when the tide ebbed. One who was on his death-bed could not find rest when the tide was in, but when it went out he went out with it. There was something in all this of the old days when Odin and Thor were worshipped where the Domkirke now stood."

More Americans go to Ribe perhaps than to any other place in Jutland, and it is not wholly on account of the outdoor play, or on account of Jacob Riis, or on account of the antiquity of the Cathedral. It is because it is such an old town, such a pretty town, and a town so unlike anything in that new world across the Atlantic to which adventuring Danes go and from which questing Americans come.

CHAPTER THREE

ENGLISH COUSINS

IF Denmark is tied to the United States by ribbons of sentiment, she is bound to England by strands so closely knit and so substantial that their histories are for long stretches one piece of fabric.

Between the years 800 to 1042, the history of one country cannot be written apart from that of the other. From 994, when Sweyn Forkbeard laid siege to London, up through 1015, when Canute the Great became master of England, up through 1801, when Lord Nelson bombarded Copenhagen, up through 1807, when the whole Danish fleet was taken to England—the two countries were acutely and constantly conscious of one another. Both were island kingdoms and both possessed colonies. Their laws and customs, methods of administration, and habits of thought were so similar that they quarrelled like cousins. They paused now and then to exchange amenities, as when England sent little Caroline Matilde over to be the unwilling bride of Christian VII and Denmark sent the beautiful Princess Alexandra to be Queen of England.

During all these visible changes, the invisible exchange of

language has been shuttling back and forth. In English place names the "by" and the "holm" derive from Danish (a by-law is a town law) and Danish signs, *Hold Fast med Venstre Haand* and *Spytning Forbudt,* need no translation. Over shop windows *hatte* and *sokker* would be comprehensible even if a row of hats or socks below did not verify one's guess, although a *bad massage* holds an awful premonition. While there are many words which, if not identical, are comprehensible in Danish and English, it is said that fishermen on the coast of Scotland can actually converse with fishermen from Jutland. Certainly the Danish *kirke, hjem,* and *barn* are even more similar to the Scottish kirk, hame, and bairn when spoken than when written. While such comparisons are endlessly fascinating, it is of even more general convenience that every third man, woman, or child in Copenhagen can understand a question couched in cockney or Californian, Londonese or Louisianian, and can answer it usually in correct and always in polite accents. These major issues of war and words have been accompanied by minor ones. British athletics, British books, British styles—Copenhagen is second only to London in its tailors—British music hall artists, are all popular in Denmark, and the English church of St. Alban's, whose corner-stone was laid by the Prince of Wales before he became Edward VII, is filled by English residents and visitors.

The centuries have wheeled their cycles in friendliness and enmity, but always in intimacy. And today that intimacy is greater than ever before. For trade is the life blood of the modern State and although everyone knows that England is Denmark's first customer, not so many are aware that Denmark is England's third customer, and that in 1934 Denmark's industrial purchases from Britain were only slightly less than those of France and Germany. In the comparatively new city of Esbjerg, on the west coast of Jutland not far from Ribe, a remarkable moving picture—admission free—illustrates this tale.

Here every single afternoon comes in the big Diesel-motored steamer from Harwich bringing English passengers and English goods, and from here every single afternoon sets out another similar steamer taking back Danish passengers and Danish goods. It is only twenty-two hours between Harwich and Esbjerg and these four neat fleet steamers are as crowded and regular as commutation trains. The trip from Copenhagen to London via the Kiel Canal is longer and the boats are smaller, but their service is of the same reliability and the cargo, coming and going, is composed of the same items.

The boat stands with its hatches open while enormous sides of bacon, each sewed into an amorphous-looking parcel, each one precisely like every other in shape and size and weight, are stowed away, hundreds upon hundreds of them, two hundred and nineteen million kilos of them in a year! Well, we need not worry about the Englishman having his bacon for breakfast. And now, in thin strong crates of new wood, come the eggs. They come on trains, they come by motor truck, they come in wagons, they come, one begins to think, through the air like snowflakes before a gale of wind. They are received, lifted up, lowered down, stowed away with a dispatch that reveals long years of familiarity with this especial commodity. Eggs, eggs, millions of eggs—more than half a million score of eggs in a year—each one a good egg—an excellent egg—clean without and fresh within. So the Englishman has the proper accompaniment to his breakfast bacon. But just to make sure that Brother Jonathan will thoroughly enjoy his meal there are a few tons of butter and a few hundred boxes of cheese, and so the hold fills up. The hold? All the holds of the nineteen refrigerated ships of the United Steamship Company which in all weathers and all seasons travel back and forth over the North Sea to Harwich, to Dunkirk, and to London Bridge. Watching the loading of just one boat and visualizing all the other boats being similarly loaded and similarly dispatched, we begin to realize what is meant by the statement that there are only two other foreign countries (the United States and the Argentine) from which Britain takes as large an import. It is an enormous amount for a little kingdom like Denmark to export. It is also an enormous amount for a great kingdom like Britain to import.

In fact, it is such an enormous amount that every now and then a sensational English newspaper or disgruntled farmer will raise a hue and cry. "These Danish dairy products," they complain, "compete with English dairy products. Our agriculture is our oldest, most heavily taxed, most under-capitalized, and most depressed industry. Why subject it to the further disadvantage of Danish competition?"

But coal is also one of England's most depressed industries, and to watch the English coal piling up in Danish yards, to watch the English steel for Danish boats and bridges being unloaded, to watch parts for motor cars and bicycles swinging from hatch to dock, is to realize what is meant by the statement that the bulk of Danish foreign imports comes from England and to realize the economic importance of the treaty of 1933 by which she agreed to purchase 80 per cent of her coal from Britain. (This agreement has been renewed for an indefinite period.) In this connexion may be quoted the surprising statement of the Central Council of the Economic

League that "Scandinavia as a whole is not only Britain's best customer in Europe but also, with the sole exception of India, our best market in the whole world."

And so, while the economists argue and the merchants dicker and the Danish-British Association produces tables based on the reports of the Board of Trade, and the British Import Union publishes a journal and the Council of Foreign Relations in London draws graphs, a few facts emerge quite definitely. Denmark is in the sterling group, as is Britain, and like Britain she has a stable economic system free from undue political influence. Each needs the other's trade and goodwill. As long as England has great industrial production and Denmark great agricultural production, there will be an exchange of goods between the two countries, with its running accompaniment of treaties and agreements—and disagreements—and the conviction, no less constant for being inconsistent, that somehow the other side always has the advantage.

While the economic relations between Denmark and England vary in cordiality with varying supply and demand, the social relations between the two are delightful. All Danes, who have enough money, go to England at least once during a lifetime. And all English people, who have enough sense, go to Denmark as often as they can. During the summer, boatloads of vacationists come along with the tinplate and textiles to Esbjerg, and many of them, as soon as they leave the big boat, step directly on a little one and ferry over to the island of Fanö.

Fanö is a small island, but it has a beach ten miles long and hard enough for motor cars to race on, as Sir Malcolm Campbell found out years ago when he was tearing over it at such speed that all four tires of all four wheels whizzed off and spun into the hinterland at exactly the same velocity as the car which continued on its rims. One of these circles of speed hit and killed a boy standing near—fantastic destiny of a soulless spectacle. Since then new methods of fastening tires to rims have been discovered, although few better beaches for racing are likely to be found anywhere.

Although the motors and bicycles fly up and down the sands, they do not interfere with the leisurely horse who, with one small boy at his head and a smaller one on his back, pulls the bathing houses, which are on wheels, first to the edge of the retreating water and then out of reach of its advance. For Fanö is not in the tideless Baltic but on the North Sea, and despite its usual sunshine and pleasant breezes, one may be inopportunely reminded of this fact by a howling gale. But the storm which drives the bathers out of the water and the bathing chairs off the beach, and sends the golfers and tennis players scuttling back to the hotel, is welcomed by the Fanö natives who know where to look for the amber which is washed up at these times and begin hunting for the semi-precious chunks and lumps as soon as enough daylight seeps through the clouds. Time was when amber was so common on the beaches of Denmark that it was used for fuel, but now it has become a rarity and is made into jewellery and combined as decoration with silver and carved wood.

Fanö has done well with accommodations and amusements for summer visitors, but its special attractions lie where they are least advertised—across the dunes and along the sandy road, past the grounds where they used to trap wild duck, past the colony where the sea-gulls nest, past rolling heath land, its purple sweep composed of infinitesimal blooms as coral reefs are composed of insects—each one a separate entity.

A windmill with its sails sedately turning announces the approach to the fishing village of Sönderho, with its cottages placed this way and that, with figure-heads which have been washed up on the shore over the front gates and shells from tropic waters bordering the garden beds, and pebbles from the beach edging the garden walks, and even mines, netted out of the North Sea, used as doubtful decorations.

Down by the beach is the "Bourse"—a long wooden bench where the sea captains used to sit and settle the affairs of the world beyond Fanö—even beyond Denmark. Out of the white-curtained doll houses which pass for human habitations peep women in native costumes, and down the crooked lanes amble artists with their paints and canvases. An occasional motor filled with summer visitors from Nordby shoves through the narrow streets without attracting any particular interest, for Fanö folk consider their own affairs quite as important and decidedly more interesting than those of sightseers.

Just what those affairs are is not so evident as it was when as many as a hundred and fifty big sailing ships went out from Fanö in a year and when there were six navigation schools and seven building yards on this small island. Now there are only four navigation schools in Denmark (in Copenhagen, Svendborg, Marstal, and Nordby), but they are large enough to take care of the applicants. Four years at sea as able-bodied seaman are required before a youth can enter such a school. He must then take a three-year course and six months on a sailing ship of sixty tons or more, which explains why Danish sailors know their business and Danish ships keep their admirable reputation on the oceans of the world.

The last of the ships which were built in Fanö were sent to the bottom by submarines. Now, to see a vessel fashioned by Fanö hands, one must go to the church which, like all churches whose worshippers are seafaring men and their families, is hung with models made by sailors on long voyages and brought home as offerings of gratitude for their safe return— or possibly as tokens of vanity in their handiwork. Among the ships suspended from the ceiling is one which drifted ashore on a smuggler's vessel, stuffed with tea, thus to end its lawless life in the odour of sanctity.

The church at Sönderho was built in 1782 and out in the graveyard the Petersens, Nielsens, and Jensens lie with anchors and crosses above them and bleeding hearts and pansies over them and two or three wives alongside. It was an unwritten law that a man should marry his deceased wife's sister and the gravestones testify that some of the widowers ran through a trio or a quartet before they embarked upon their last voyage.

The pews in the church came from Ribe Cathedral thirty years ago. They are blue-green like the sea, with a painted brown-and-white line like a strand of seaweed. On one of the chandeliers the bobèches are in the shape of scallop shells, and the little ships sailing in the air above the heads of the congregation might be sailing on an invisible sea. It was just such a "little grey church on a windy shore" that the most English of English poets must have had in mind when his forsaken merman heard

> "Through the surf and through the swell,
> The far-off sound of a silver bell."

In just such a place he

> ". . . went up the beach, by the sandy down
> Where the sea-stocks bloom, to the white-wall'd town."

And

". . . climb'd on the graves, on the stones worn with rains,
And . . . gazed up the aisle through the small leaded panes."

English ballads and Danish ballads are much alike—so very
much alike that one speculates if the "lily white hand" of the
former may not once have been the *"lille hvide haand"* of the
latter.

The sea, the church, and the little ships swinging from the
ceiling—on the island of Fanö as on the island of Aran one
finds this trinity. For seafaring folk are mystics and neither in
Denmark nor in England do they draw sharp distinctions as
to where the watery element ends and the heavenly element
begins.

CHAPTER FOUR

BATTLE-FIELDS

THE Rebild hills in central Jutland are associated with
America, and the port of Esbjerg on the west coast is associated with England, but South Jutland is associated with
Germany—not so happily as in the two first instances. Frontier
territory, especially in congested Europe, always has peculiar
problems, and that which lies between Denmark and Germany is no exception.

It is strewn with evidences of the wars between these two
neighbours who are too close geographically and too dissim-
ilar temperamentally. One cannot help being conscious that
although the Slesvig-Holstein question is nominally settled,
there is a tension in this part of Denmark which exists nowhere else in the kingdom. There is no necessity for the average traveller to wade through the endless intricacies which, as
Lord Palmerston once remarked, had been understood by
only three persons in the world. One was the Prince Consort
who was dead, one was a German judge who was in an insane
asylum, and the third was Lord Palmerston himself who had
forgotten it. Without competing with this trio we may, never-

theless, sort out one or two facts which will help to interpret the appearance and atmosphere of this region.

Until about 1110 the region of Holstein—which had been a fief of the Germano-Roman Empire—formed part of the duchy of Saxony. It was made a duchy in 1472. From 1460 to 1864, it was ruled by members of the House of Oldenburg, some of whom were also Kings of Denmark. When King Frederik VII of Denmark died (November 1863) he left no male heirs and the question arose whether the duchy was or was not an integral part of Denmark with which it had been intimately associated for centuries.

The duchy of Slesvig, on the other hand, had, since time immemorial, been a Danish fief. It was the most Danish of Danish provinces and all its legislation since 1241 had been based upon the laws of the Danish King Valdemar.

A bright boy of twelve might have figured out that instead of fighting over the two duchies for generations, it would have been simpler to let Germany have Holstein and Denmark have Slesvig. But nations are not so sensible as twelve-year-old boys. Germany and Denmark agreed on just one point: that the two duchies were "indissoluble." The Eider Danes, claiming Slesvig as an integral part of the Danish kingdom, insisted upon the retention of Holstein also. The Germans, claiming Holstein as part of Germany, insisted upon Slesvig.

These irreconcilable claims resulted, quite naturally, in insurrections, provisional government, plebiscites, and all sorts of proselytizing within the duchies, in bitter and costly wars between Germany and Denmark and in an attendant furore of protests, interventions, guarantees, conferences, and partisanship on the part of Austria, England, Sweden, and Russia. In 1864 Germany won Slesvig and Holstein and held them until 1919, during which time she completed the Kiel Canal. The Treaty of Versailles gave back to Denmark the northern part of Slesvig. Southern Slesvig and Holstein belong to Germany.

Whoever wishes to believe that during the time the duchies belonged to Germany the Danish population was justly treated, that the plebiscite was honestly and the language question fairly managed, and that the Slesvig-Holsteiners were loyal Germans, has only to read any German history. And whoever wishes to believe that the present German minority in Slesvig is given every generous consideration, that the language question is so handled as to satisfy the German-speaking Slesvigers, has only to ask any Dane.

It all might seem like ancient history to anyone neither Danish nor German, but as soon as one enters South Jutland from Sönderborg, the battle-fields extend over such large areas that the past begins to gather a substantiality—or at least an emotional actuality.

A new Dybböl windmill stands upon the site and reconstructs the form of the original which was twice destroyed and twice rebuilt during the fightings and bombardments which centred around this coveted rise of ground. Historians, antiquarians, patriots, and trippers swarm over the redoubts, spell out inscriptions, and visit the museum beside the windmill which preserves pictures of boy soldiers, bearded like the pard, the torn flags and stained uniforms, the weapons and diaries— all the sad and bloody paraphernalia of those sad and bloody years. Everywhere are cannon-balls and graves of German dead and Danish dead—all old bones now—and maps to show the visitor where to walk and where to look for memorial stones and sites of obliterated buildings.

1864—the date when the provinces were annexed by Germany—is still in everyone's mouth, as is 1920, the date when fifty thousand Danes crowded on the redoubts to see King Christian X on a white horse ride over the old frontier, receive a flag from the old man who offered it, embrace him, and thus formally take possession of the territory which had been lost. Not so many were present to see the King in Tiprup Church take off his cap, kneel and bend his head in a prayer of thanksgiving.

The new Dybböl windmill turns its sails and grinds its grain as placidly as its predecessors. But the sunshine has a melancholy tinge for whoever raises his eyes from the Broager memorial stones with the names of a hundred and ninety dead and from the pointed twin spires of the Broager Church which for eight hundred years has glorified the Prince of Peace, and sees the roofs of the new barracks built to hold two thousand soldiers.

For South Jutland is not merely an historical region romanticized by

> *"Old, unhappy, far-off things,*
> *And battles long ago."*

It is still a part of the mainland of Europe, and it is still geographically a part of Germany. When one is on its soil it is impossible not to feel the pressure of a restless and inimical world against its border.

Something of the atmosphere and heavier architecture of a Rhine town is immediately apparent in the city of Sönderborg on its little island of Als, separated from Jutland by the deep narrow Alssund and connected to it by one of those handsome new bridges in which Denmark is so prodigal and so proficient.

Even the castle built by Valdemar the Great and Archbishop Absalon eight centuries ago suggests a continental stronghold. In this castle one of the most interesting figures in Danish history—King Christian II—was imprisoned for seventeen years, and the flagstones worn by his incessant pacing around and around the table show how he spent that fearful time. This romantic lover, this enlightened humanist who loved to converse with Erasmus, Dürer, Lucas Cranach, and Luther; this man of theories who imported two hundred Dutch peasants to the island of Amager to teach the Danes agriculture—it is still the market garden of Copenhagen— spent twenty-seven years of his seventy-seven in prison. His execution of Swedish nobles for alleged treason led to wars, but his theories for substituting a benevolent socialism for the power of the clergy and the nobility do not sound so dangerous or so crazy to the Danes of the twentieth century as they did to those of the sixteenth.

South Jutland—Sönderjylland, as the Danes call it, and North Slesvig, as it is marked on old maps—is definitely borderland, and gains, from that very fact, a certain interest for the stranger.

In the Graasten Church—which is connected with Graasten Castle, within whose dignified white walls the Crown Prince and Princess spend a part of every year—a German pastor once a month holds the Lutheran service in German, and the church itself is German baroque. Near Aabenraa are more barracks—new ones—and officers are quartered in the Castle.

Aabenraa is ventilated by breezes from the wider world. It has been, ever since the captains used to sail out of the harbour in their own vessels bound for China. Most of the population of this old shipping town still gets its living from the

sea, but in a different way from centuries ago to judge by the
steamers unloading coal from England and the ships coming
in under sail with lumber from Sweden or Finland. Generations of sea captains' wives and sailors' widows have lived in
these houses whose bay windows overlook the water and they
have become familiar with visitations not only from foreign
countries but from the elements, as the flood marks of 1871
upon the Custom-House prove. The men of Aabenraa are accustomed to dealing with men across the border, for electrical
power from here is sent not only all through South Jutland
but to Germany.

At Aabenraa one begins to understand why South Jutland-
ers have a distinctive point of view. International problems
are close to them. If they are a bit more stern than other
Danes, they feel themselves less provincial. It is not merely
that Germany is to the south. Europe lies beyond the frontier.
The roads are not only military thoroughfares but commercial
ones as well, and have resounded to the hooves of cattle being
driven to foreign markets even more often than to the sound
of the feet of foreign soldiers. Cattle are international coin
and in a hamlet like Kliplev every house becomes a public
house when cattle dealers come to town, and small-town men
acquire large-town ideas—even ideas of a world beyond Denmark.

The human vibrations in South Jutland are different from
those in other parts of Denmark, and different, too, from the
forest and farms of Zealand and from the sands and heaths
of Jutland are those filmy leagues of plain which roll away
into the veiled distances and are lost in mirage. This frontier
land has no topographical frontier. An invisible line is drawn
from Flensborg to the North Sea running out into the ocean

between the islands of Sylt and Römö. The line lies across
the highway and is guarded by uniformed Customs officers,
and it lies across the back yards and is guarded by a few potato
plants, and it lies through woodland where there is apparently
no guard at all. It cuts cottages in half and it severs the alle-
giances of those inhabitants who are Danish-born and German-
minded, or who are German in speech but Danish at heart.

The province of Slesvig has belonged to Denmark for centuries and belonged to Germany for fifty-four years. During those fifty-four years German was not only the official language, but Danish was prohibited in courts of law, the clergy
had to be educated in Kiel and the teachers trained in the
Fatherland. Today, although only 13 per cent of the population is German, this minority has a representative in the Folketing and there is a German-speaking school wherever there are
as many—or as few—as ten German-speaking children, the Danish Government contributing sixty-four kroner yearly for each
pupil. There are fifty-four such schools in Slesvig and Germany will lend money to Danes on condition that they send
their children to them.

The German impress is evident not only in the spoken language and printed street signs in Tönder, but in the architecture. While Tönder has its share of one-story cottages, it is
less doll-like than many other Danish cities. The substantial
two-, three-, and four-story buildings are tall and handsome
with ornate ironwork, deeply carved woodwork, and laborious
fancy brickwork. Street signs of great size are suspended from
elaborate iron brackets, blue-and-white tiles decorate the outside of bay windows which hang over or crowd out upon the
sidewalks. There are more men smoking meerschaum pipes,
more dachshunds padding down the streets. German titles

are over many of the shops, and the names of all the streets are given in both languages. Near the German-speaking school there is a monument to Kaiser Wilhelm I. Even the hand-woven woollen goods from the famous weaving school are tinged with the chocolate browns and purplish reds of Germany, although the Tönder lace—which home industry is be-ing revived—is still delicately Danish.

There is a continual passing back and forth between the two countries. Germans come across the border to open a newspaper and hunt out the items whose publication is prohibited at home. German Jews are advertising for Danish wives, for such alliances make it easier to settle in a country which, since the days of Georg Brandes, has been willing to recognize genius and value intelligence even in a Hebrew. Recently Jews have come up from Germany to study agriculture in Denmark before going to Palestine to settle.

Just as Tönder with its columned doorways and baroque gables differs from lighter, whiter Danish towns, so does the countryside around it differ in general effect. This is partly because the bricks, made of a native clay, are of a darker, more sombre brown, almost the same colour as the brown thatched roofs; and it is partly because many of the houses and barns are on artificially raised grounds on account of the spring floods.

These spring floods are held back now by a double series of dikes, and although these dikes are high enough and substantial enough to protect the countryside they are not so high as to destroy its peculiar shimmering enchantment. The two windmills of Höjer are sentinels for that lightly pencilled expanse. Storks are their patrol. There is a special herbage which grows on land deluged by spring floods, and when the dike

was raised in Ribe and the floods no longer soaked the plain
the herbage changed. But it still grows on these insubstantial
acres which lie between the dikes and the River Vidå to the
west of Tönder, and on it, as far as the eye can see, sheep, like
little curls of cloud, graze upon that inverted sky which is "a
playground for the winds: a floor for the light of evening to
flow along, the home of mirage and coloured airs." Beyond
these swimming leagues dartled with rivulets lies the water,
and on the water float the islands of Sylt and Römö, one of
them German, one of them Danish. Beyond them all, to the
south, "there ariseth a little cloud out of the sea, like a man's
hand"—Germany.

It would not be fair to imply that this borderland has always
had a home-loving peaceable nation on one side and the pushing greedy continent on the other. In the days when Denmark
was young and lusty she took the offensive; she pressed down
into the south; she invaded and marauded. And the road she
hewed out is still to be seen and is still traversable.

It is a flat and treeless road, stretching for four or five kilometres through meadows: an unpaved, sleepy track, rutted by
wheels, with other ruts on either side showing that in muddy
weather carts—and courageous motors—sheer over to the grass.
People may tell you it is the old ox path, by which cattle used
to be driven down from Jutland into Germany, and so it is.
They may add it is an ancient military way, and this, too, is
easy to believe, looking at the map and seeing how narrow is
the neck by which Denmark can be entered, overland, from
Europe. But they may not tell you—and if they do it is not so
immediately easy to comprehend—that this is the oldest road
in the world still in its original state and still in constant use.
For unlike the paved Roman highways—which have been un-

earthed on various far-flung terrains—this road has never been lost, obliterated, fallen into disuse, or suffered a repair or alteration. It draws its length from before recorded history, and it extends into a future beyond the dream of anyone now living, for it is forbidden that it shall be in any way changed or used for any purpose other than a common thoroughfare.

This very road, so passively spread between level meadows, bore its past in the migration of the tribes; doubtless it was first forced open and trampled down by those savage hordes whose records are like shadows, obscure but undeniable.

Over these rutted tracks two thousand years ago the Cimbrians poured forth, driven out of North Jutland by rising floods. Huge, red, bristling warriors, with their wives, children, and thralls; with their wagons—one of which carried the sacred bronze bull, and the ancestral fire, tended by vestal virgins and sibylline priestesses—with their bullocks and small tough horses—proceeding slowly so that the herds could graze their way—irresistibly drawn southward to try their scythe-like swords against the legions of Marius.

The sacred bronze bull, with the wooden idol secreted within it, was to be captured at Vercelli (in 101 B.C.); the brawny barbarian men were to perish in gladiatorial barracks at Pompeii or walk in chains along the Via Sacra before the triumphal chariot of Marius; and the women, taller, whiter than any the South had seen before, were to be sold in the slave market in Rome. But when the vast swarm, blue-eyed and sunburnt, came thundering and roistering down this way, they dreamed only of glory in the unknown land beyond the Alps.

After the Cimbrians, men and beasts, marching through the long story of mankind, have continually pushed up this road to the North, ebbed down it to the South. Pagans, clad in animal skins and carrying their idols; knights clad in armour and carrying the Cross; soldiers in bullet-proof helmets, carrying gas bombs—they have all sweated and struggled along this route, so that today as we motor slowly along its length the green fields on either side redden into torrents of blood, and the air is heavy with racial memories that lie too deep for logical thought.

No, Denmark was not always the well-controlled and sensible country she is today. For almost a thousand years her history was a chronicle of battles, sieges, treaties made and treaties broken, bravery on one side and duplicity on the other—dependent on whether one is reading Danish history, or Swedish, German, English, Austrian, or Russian. It is a chronicle of quarrelling and fighting with every single country in Europe except France, of blood-letting on land and sea, offensives and defensives, suffering, glory, heroism, and waste, with breathing spells in which Denmark reflects that war is futile and the ways of peace are ways of blessedness.

The prehistoric, the heroic, the Viking periods; the invasion and conquering of England (which may be traced in the outline at the back of the book) brought Denmark, during the Middle Ages, to the hegemony of the North. In area the smallest of the Scandinavian countries, she was the most powerful. When the domination of the Hanseatic cities threatened to crush her, and when in other civil feuds she became demoralized, Valdemar Atterdag restored her to her pristine position. His daughter Margaret was one of the most remarkable sovereigns Europe has ever known. The great chronicle of Lübeck said of her: "When men saw the wisdom and strength that were in this royal lady wonder and fear filled their hearts."

It was she who brought about the union of the three Scandinavian kingdoms. Her empire, which reached northward from the Gulf of Finland to the Varanger Fjord on the Polar Seas and southward to the Eider, and included the islands of Orkney, Shetland, Iceland, and Greenland in the Atlantic, was the most extensive monarchy in Europe. It embraced territory twice that of the German Empire. But although Norway, Sweden, and Denmark were thus nominally combined, it was a dynastic union—not a true union of three peoples—for Denmark continued to be the predominating power and to rule the other two countries in her own interest. The Danish-Norwegian union lasted for more than four hundred years— from 1397 until the surrender of Norway to Sweden in 1814. The Danish-Swedish union lasted nominally a little over a hundred and twenty years—until 1523.

But union or no union, Denmark and Sweden, before they reached their present urbane maturity, were tussling about provinces on land and passages through the sea in wars and battles that cover endless pages of history. Denmark's relations with England have simmered down to cousinly exchange. Denmark and Germany are two neighbours, not fundamentally congenial but trying to make the best of their proximity. But Denmark and Sweden are like blood brothers who, after an infancy of grabbing each other's rattles, an adolescence of scuffling for each other's kites and tops, a young manhood of circumventing each other in the acquisition of desirable house lots, have finally come into friendly, even affectionate, middle age. They have learned not only how to behave but how to enjoy the give and take of mature intercourse. They recall their mutual warfare with mutual good humour, and although they are not above taking a sly crack now and then at each other's idiosyncrasies they, as nations, exercise the same good behaviour in their social dealings and good judgment in their business dealings as rational and intelligent individuals.

While this forbearance, this determination to solve any issue by compromise, is most evident between Denmark and Sweden who are so close geographically, it is true of all five Scandinavian countries, even with Norway which is inclined to be a bit prickly, even with Finland which has Baltic as well as Scandinavian affiliations. Such a unique and civilized solidarity is worthier of study than the wars which preceded it—wars like all others—born of greed, kept alive by blood transfusions, finally degenerating into death and being commemorated by epithets of falsehood.

Although these wars are not, for the layman, worth detailed study, they yielded many episodes which have been the stock-in-trade for painters and poets and the writers of historical romances ever since. One of the popular stories is of Peter Tordenskjold who, off Cape Lindeness in 1714, after battling for hours with a Swedish vessel, ran out of gunpowder. He sent a messenger over to the enemy vessel to explain that he would be obliged to let it escape, but that he hoped, before the Commander sailed away, he would come on board and drink a toast. The Swedish Commander declined haughtily. Therefore Tordenskjold manœuvred close alongside and asked to borrow some gunpowder so he could continue fighting. This so amused the Commander that he mounted to the quarter-deck and holding a goblet of wine in his hand drank a toast to the audacious Tordenskjold who also raised his goblet. Thus terminated this sea fight.

But the favourite story of all is that of Charles X of Sweden who (1658) marched across the Little Belt on the ice under cover of darkness and suddenly fell upon the Danes who were as astonished as if he had leaped down from the clouds. Even today, when they point out the spot marked by old cannon, where the Swedes landed, they smile in remembrance of the utter amazement of their own troops and in something very like admiration for the boldness of the Swedes.

This spot was on Fünen, the island which lies between Zealand and Jutland, and, oddly enough, it is in the grounds of a club for the furtherance of friendly understanding and closer cultural relations among the five Scandinavian countries. Norden, as this club is called, was founded in 1919 and its fifteen hundred members have branches in Denmark, Sweden, Finland, Norway, and Iceland. The headquarters are in Hindsgavl, a quite magnificent old château, where in 1814 the Treaty of Kiel was signed. With its lawns and bathing beach, its woods and park-like grounds and its accommodation for a hundred guests, Hindsgavl, no longer a private dwelling, lends itself admirably to this international sociability.

Here during the summer come for a few days or a fortnight college professors, grandmothers, sea captains, widows, athletic boys, young business and professional men, writers, artists, social workers, fathers, mothers, and children. They come from various parts of Denmark and from the four other Scandinavian countries. They have lectures and conferences, but the distinctive feature of Norden is its friendly informality. Here in one of the spacious panelled rooms an Icelander chats with a Dane. Swedish children run up and down the double stairway in the great white Empire hall. A Norwegian and a Dane argue about Greenland. In front of a pavilion where Hans Christian Andersen used to sit, and which is piously roped off, a Finnish boy races a Swede to the beach where they will both take a swim.

During the long summer days they go on picnics and walks, and in the short evening they gather in the drawing-room and read aloud, or sing together, or make up their own entertainment.

The atmosphere at Hindsgavl is truly remarkable. It is like an immense old-fashioned family reunion whose members have become widely scattered, but who have now reached that period in life when they begin to revalue their common heritage and to realize that even though they have been pursuing different lines of thought and activity, nevertheless they are kin, and that it is good to meet and affirm their kinship.

The purpose of Norden is moral and intellectual, but the manner of carrying this out is easy and breezy and without cant. An aristocratic air still stamps the architecture and furnishing of Hindsgavl, but simplicity marks the living of its present democratically inclined occupants. There is no austerity. Scandinavians are not Puritans, and all of them—from Norway and Finland, and from Iceland and Sweden—appreciate good food and good fun as well as good conversation.

If it is appropriate that Norden should have its headquarters on the spot where the Danes and the Swedes once fought, it is also appropriate that such a centre of friendliness and good humour should be on Fünen. For Fünen is the fondly regarded "middle daughter" between the bigger sisters of Zealand and Jutland; a darling daughter, a daughter with a singing voice, all smiles and dimples and gaiety. Happy the traveller who directs his steps and face to her.

CHAPTER FIVE

BRIDGES, BOATS, AND TOURISTS

A KINGDOM which is composed of islands has naturally become adept in bridge building. Island dwellers, surrounded by coasts indented with harbours, have naturally become sailors and boat builders. A country which is situated in Europe and surrounded by navigable waters has naturally been, since earliest time, a sea trader.

Denmark spins bridges from island to island with the facility of a spider flinging webs from grass tip to grass tip. It is to be expected that Falster and Lolland should be thus connected, and that Amager should be practically a part of Copenhagen. But when a bridge with a total length of twelve hundred metres was built across the Little Belt and another—the longest in Europe—spans the Storström between Zealand and Falster—it is something else again. Now there is talk of a bridge of seventeen and a half kilometres across the Great Belt (between Zealand and Fünen) where the depth of the water presents problems entirely new to engineering, and there is—and has been for some years—an even more spectacular project of a bridge between Denmark and the Scandinavian Peninsula, which presents problems for the politician as well as for the engineer.

In a country of independent thinkers, talkers, and doers, where discussion is free and fashionable, everyone has his theory about this latter. It should go between Elsinore (in Denmark) and Helsingborg (in Sweden) at the entrance to the Sound. It should be placed further to the south and be supported midway by the island of Hven. It should go between Copenhagen and Malmö and be fourteen kilometres long with supports on the islands of Amager and Saltholm. All of these projects and all the ideas about them and all the calculations involving ten years of time and hundreds of millions of kroner should be dismissed for ever. This passion for bridge building, like Egypt's passion for pyramid building, is grandiose and useless. Denmark doesn't need any more bridges, it doesn't need those it has. Ferry boats did very well across the Little Belt and one enjoyed the journey as if it were an ocean trip. Ferry boats are entirely adequate for all Danish-Swedish commuting.

But the ayes seem to have it. The Viking instinct in every male to launch a boat and put out to sea at all seasons and in any direction has been transmuted into the more complicated but still persistent instinct of the Danes to construct bridges even if they must be of reinforced concrete with steel super-structure and railway tracks and motor ways, and to build boats even if these are driven by Diesel engines instead of by sail. Engineers want to design bridges and boats, employers of labour want to build them, and far-sighted economists and near-sighted business men all want to facilitate travel not only within the borders of the country but to those borders from all over the world, and through them from the Continent to the Scandinavian Peninsula.

Ever since the State College of Engineering was founded

(1829) it has turned out engineers of such ability that they have been in demand throughout Europe. They have built railways in Persia and Turkey, and railway and street bridges in Lithuania, and cement works in Siam, Egypt, England, Canada, India, China, and Japan. They have constructed important harbour works in Funchal, Madeira, and Corunna, Spain, and most conspicuous of all, in Gdynia, Poland. In 1924 this was a fishing hamlet of six hundred and it is now a port of sixty thousand inhabitants.

The founder of the State College of Engineering—and also its first principal—was H. C. Oersted, the discoverer of electromagnetism, and the institution which started with twenty-two pupils now has over a thousand, and graduates a hundred and twenty yearly. Although about 10 per cent of these are employed in foreign lands, Denmark herself has need for the rest, if all the five hundred islands are to be linked together and all the five score harbours to be kept busy with departing and arriving vessels and every vessel to be equipped with a Danish-built Diesel engine!

The Lillebaeltsbro which connects the mainland of Jutland to the island of Fünen is the first of Denmark's great bridges to be traversed by the foreigner who lands at Esbjerg, and saves him four hours on the trip from London to Copenhagen. Although engineers come from distant lands to study the way in which the problem of an exceptionally strong current and exceptionally deep water has been met, the untechnical traveller sees, rather, the fairylike filament swinging over a miniature sea and leaping past an island whose spires dissolve like soap bubbles against the light of the sky. (They tell us this fanciful edifice is a Girls' Reform School, but we don't believe it unless they are Charlotte Mew changelings, "not quite bad and not quite good" who must "grow up but never grow old" and who "never come back again.")

Such an aerial span is quite the proper approach to Fünen, where the fields seem more flowery and the speech more lilting than elsewhere in Denmark and where even the solid capital—Odense—embodies the practical and the playful in the best national tradition.

For the city to which forty thousands of people come yearly to see the house where a writer of fairy-tales was born bristles with engineers and naval architects, and the fourth largest harbour in Denmark resounds to the noise of pneumatic steel riveting and welding.

The ship-yards in Odense, like those throughout the country, turn out vessels in about half the time required in other countries, because foremen and workmen understand their business and understand each other. Such speedy and such excellent work gives employment to twelve thousand men and places Denmark fourth among the ship-building countries of the world, preceded only by Great Britain, Germany, and Japan—such an astonishing statement that one turns to Lloyd's Register for confirmation.

These Danish-built ships are used by Danish companies for carrying freight and passengers from one Danish port to another, and so great is this traffic by water among the islands that two million tons of goods—not counting what is carried by the ferries—are transported annually. The United Steamship Company alone can, in its colonial service, book three thousand passengers in a day, and if it stopped for twenty-four hours Denmark would lose three million kroner. Besides this inter-Danish port traffic the greater part of the goods shipped from Denmark to foreign countries is carried in

Danish-built bottoms, and the Danish flag is familiar in the harbours of Asia, Africa, and Australia as well as North and South America. Finally, the Danish Mercantile Marine with its tramps and tankers and regular liners holds an extremely important place in the international carrying trade that does not touch at Denmark. The Maersk Line, for instance, has forty steamers, motor vessels, and tankers, trading the world over, besides its half a dozen big motor ships for passengers between the United States and the Far East. Some of these forty are old-fashioned freighters, some are comfortable passenger-cargo steamers, and the newest are Diesel-motored, with strong rooms, silk rooms, refrigerated holds and tanks especially constructed for transporting delicate oils. In fact, so immense is the traffic in the international carrying trade that two-thirds of the money earned by the Danish Mercantile Marine comes from the trade between foreign ports and one-third from that between foreign and Danish ports.

Denmark knows how to build ships, how to man them, and how to run them economically, efficiently, on schedule, and without Government subsidy, which they resolutely refuse, and she manages to pay officers and crew higher wages than any other country except the United States. At present she has no direct passenger line between the United States and Denmark, but throws her interest into the Polish line—the Gdynia-America—whose boats run regularly between New York and Gdynia, stopping at Copenhagen.

The blue waters of the Öresund are still bright with sails, but while some of these are barques and brigantines and square-riggers, the majority are small pleasure boats. For there are no new cargo-carrying sailing ships being built in Denmark today, although a few old timers are still in use. And as sail was superseded by steam, steam is being succeeded by the motor.

The first motor ship in the world was the *Selandia* of the East Asiatic Company and when, in 1912, she made her way across the North Sea and up the Thames without sails, without steam, and without tugboats, Winston Churchill, then Cabinet Minister, came down to welcome her. It was, however, years before the cautious Britishers ordered their first Diesel ship. In the meantime, Denmark kept perfecting this method of transportation, which was her unique invention. On motor ships all over the seven seas one reads the name of Burmeister and Wain, the firm which converted the Diesel engine, which was originally stationary, into a marine engine, thus making possible long voyages without the loss of time in stopping for, or the loss of space in storing, fuel. The engineers of Denmark, working with those of other countries, have invented several types of Diesel marine engines, so that today not only large vessels but small fishing craft may be thus economically and efficiently equipped. The Danish characteristic of willingly accepting new inventions and labour-saving devices is well exemplified in her general acceptance of the Diesel marine engine. The largest and most modern of the State ferries are driven by Diesel engines and the entire fleet of the East Asiatic Company, which is the second largest in the kingdom, is made up of motor ships. Norway alone is as progressive as Denmark in substituting motor power for steam.

The Odense Steel Shipbuilding Company is one of the largest in Denmark. Out in the river, motor vessels, tankers, and freighters for Danish and for foreign trade are being constructed within sight of the spot where an optimist is raising bananas and pineapples under glass. While the practical value of such an operation may be compared to raising Arctic whales in the Philippines in refrigerated water so that the Filipinos would not need to import whale oil, its accomplishment should give satisfaction to those advocates of high tariff who argue that every country should produce everything it needs. When this has been carried to its logical finale, there will be no more need for ships or—happy thought—for tariffs!

In the meantime, Odense is so prosperous, and the men employed in the ship-yards maintain such a comfortable standard of living in houses they have purchased from the Company and which would be suitable to a first-class American suburb, that the local income tax is only 5 per cent or 6 per cent, in contrast to the 20 per cent of some other Danish cities.

Despite its ancient landmarks—such as the tomb of St. Canute, grand-nephew of Canute the Great, and despite its very name, Odin's City, which recalls its extreme age—the capital of Fünen is an up-to-date metropolis with seventy-five thousand inhabitants and an opera season and, a little way out, an observation tower which is, after the Eiffel, the highest in Europe. There are elevators in the spider-web structure to a restaurant near the top and although foreigners are among those who ride or climb to the dizzy look out, most of the sight-seers who take this opportunity to survey more of Denmark are Danes.

They look out with pride over the boats and bridges linking the water to the land and with approval at the railway tracks, State-owned, and carrying the super-modern Diesel electric streamlined trains and at the network of roads connecting town to town. There is need of all these highways and by-ways, for Denmark takes first place among the countries of the Continent in number of motor vehicles per capita besides those which holiday makers from other lands bring with them.

These roads are well made, well kept and well marked, and in such a gently contoured terrain may be traversed from dawn to dark without shifting gears. However, strangers who think it would be "fun to knock about Denmark in a little motor" will soon discover that such fun may not be indulged in more than sixty kilometres an hour and that "knocking about" after having had a few Danish *snaps* may end not in a mere reprimand, not in a mere revoking of a licence, but in a prison sentence, and neither does this have to be conditioned by an accident! The right-hand drive is a convenience to Americans and an inconvenience to Englishmen and the bicycles are a nuisance to them both, so it is well to be philosophical and law-abiding when motoring through these mild meadows and through hamlets which, although ancient, are not decrepit, and which, although friendly, refuse being too rudely exploited. The Danes, looking out from the Odense Tower, are accustomed to give and receive consideration and intend to keep their heritage unspoiled.

For there never were any people who loved their country more devotedly and artlessly. They love it not with the strident self-assertion of patriots of a new land, or of an old land being newly organized; not with the melancholy of a people who feel their established empire disintegrating in an unpredictable age. No, the Danes unaffectedly delight in their gay cities and frankly adore their farms and fields. As for their homes —their motto might be not "My God and my country" but "My country and my home." For the trimmed hedges and trees and swept walks about the big house, the little house—

and the pigsty and the barn for that matter—are evidences of enjoyment rather than of perfunctory tidiness. The most attractive traits of Danish character are expressed at home: affection, spontaneously demonstrative, between parents and children, brothers and sisters; consideration, generous and quick, to guests. There are good temper and cosiness even in the most modest household, and humour and happy ease even in the most elaborate. Occasionally an outsider will criticize the Danes' pleasure in everything Danish as smugness. It would be truer to interpret it as a felicitous adjustment between temperament and age. For Denmark is done with the impetuosities and self-recriminations and rash heroisms of youth. Common sense, appreciation of small pleasures, refusal to bicker over small unpleasantnesses, and a readiness to laugh —these are the compensations of maturity.

The significance of any country is derived not from its hills and plains and waters but from the character of the people who have gradually and irrevocably shaped it into an entity more elusive and more enduring than any individual life. One reason why the scenery of Denmark escapes the tedium of mere prettiness and offers more than superficial gratification to the eye is that it is the visible reflection of a rational and happy nation.

The trip from Odense to Nyborg, for instance—why do these winding country roads bordered by topped poplars and skirting ponds scattered with lilies, white and yellow and red; why do these cottages, criss-crossed with espaliered cherry trees and settled into currant bushes whose smaller clusters of fruit repeat the same glint of scarlet; why do these white latticed fences with blue posts and pink roses gladden our hearts unless it is that they are symbols of thrift, simplicity, and contentment—qualities so old-fashioned as to be novel, almost piquant, in a maladjusted and neurotic world?

The seaside town of Nyborg with young people romping in the water and older people tramping in cross-country walks, and others, still older but quite as merry, pacing in the beech woods, exudes an air refreshing not entirely because of salt breezes and forest fragrance. This admirable wholesomeness, however, is not permitted to pall. For, as in the Danish character practicality is balanced by playfulness, so is the Arcadian naïveté of the scene dignified by sophistication. Everywhere in Denmark castles are thick as raisins in a cake, and in Fünen they are thick as raisins in a fruit cake—a very good fruit cake —a superior fruit cake—a fruit cake guaranteed to give satisfaction.

The grey fortress at Nyborg claiming—like how many others?—to be the oldest in Scandinavia, is sombre and masculine, stern and splendid. Outside the walls of the towers and bastions are pock-marked with age. Inside they are decorated with the original black-and-white frescoes. The Knights' Hall is as starkly intact as when the warriors of seven hundred years ago feasted within it, stamping their feet on the three-foot-wide oaken planks of the floor. They did not trouble their noble heads about the rights or wrongs of the peasants. They took it for granted that these yokels existed only to make life for the aristocracy more agreeable in peace and more glorious in war. They would have roared in merriment if someone had told them their weapons and furniture would be gathered up in a museum within these ponderous walls. One must remember these forebears to understand the sturdy Danes of today.

There are no slums around Danish cities, and the country grows
up to the town as naturally as sea sands are moulded into dunes.

ALLEGHENY COLLEGE LIBRARY

The little bronze mermaid sits on a wave-washed rock at the harbour's edge.

ALLEGHENY COLLEGE LIBRARY

Denmark, fourth among the ship-building countries of the world, knows how to run her boats without Government subsidy.

ALLEGHENY COLLEGE LIBRARY

Hans Christian Andersen's fairy stories, translated into thirty-five languages, achieve new immortality with every new generation of children.

ALLEGHENY COLLEGE LIBRARY

Kerteminde, with its fish nets drying and its fishing boats coming and going with their glittering cargo, is more than a "picturesque" beach and "quaint" main street. Manor-houses testify to activities outside those of fishing and ploughing, and burial mounds to the north give a perspective too deep to be caught by a light water-colour sketch. Although Kerteminde is sure that it is the most delightful of them all—an opinion also held by Johannes Larsen, the painter, who chooses to make it his home—there are dozens of these small villages in Fünen, equally captivating and equally undiscovered.

In the fringed coast line to the south are caught up harbours and ports and summer resorts where jollity is tossed back and forth between visiting yachts from Sweden and England and various parts of Denmark, and the castles and manor-houses on the bluff. These castles and manor-houses are in astonishing profusion and they are encompassed by a cloud of lesser, but not less delightful, residences owned or leased by people who like to enjoy life and have perfected themselves in that graceful accomplishment.

Denmark has long been the happy hunting ground for social study groups, for educators, agriculturists, political economists, and scientists. For not only is the country small enough to be surveyed in its entirety, not only are its statistics and various tabulations accurately assembled and easily accessible, but every Dane is a self-appointed host to every stranger, and the principal of a Folk High School or the superintendent of a ship-building yard will not hesitate to leave his dinner or forgo his business to show a visiting pedagogue or engineer around. In the guest books which are so meticulously kept in every public building, dairies as well as museums, one sees names from China and Russia, Egypt and Estonia, Australia and Japan. And in private homes, the humble as well as the great, similar guest books testify that there have been admitted —and more astonishingly, welcomed—sightseers whose only credentials were inquisitiveness.

The Danes are genuinely friendly and they provide visitors with more than boats and bridges to get to Denmark and more than roads and scenery after they arrive. Believing in comfort for themselves, they believe in it also for their guests. One may eat and drink delightfully in every part of the country, and the new hotels have realized that the past when the Englishman used to travel with his private portable bath tub has given place to the present when the American insists upon travelling with private porcelain-lined bathrooms. To be sure, such bathrooms often seem installed more for the convenience of the plumber than the occupants, and in rented houses landlords sometimes stipulate that if tenants wish to put in such unnecessary appendages they must take them out when they leave.

But even if Americans are not so completely encircled and confronted by plumbing as at home, modernization has come to Denmark as to the rest of the world. Those sections of not-so-old guide-books called "Serviceable Sentences for Common Use" prove it: "Where do we change horses?"; "Can you procure me a boat with a couple of rowers?"; "I shall perform the journey on horseback"—one wonders how soon "taxis," "motors," and "aeroplanes" will sound equally obsolete. Intriguing, too, are the instructions as to suitable clothing given in those volumes. "For ladies," says Murray's *Handbook of Denmark,* "the travelling dress should be of a strong fabric, Scotch spun silk or some very light woollen material. Stout boots and a pair of goloshes for wet decks are useful. For wraps, the best are a Scotch plaid, of the largest and coarsest size." (Why should the *plaid* be large? Answer, echo!) "A jacket of sealskin or cloth, and wadded; and a large cloak with sleeves and cape."

All this is as antiquated as the dodo. Danish women dress as smartly as other Continental women and there are no such things as "wet decks" unless one wants to leave the glassed verandas and go hunting for them.

There is, however, one point before which the twentieth century has halted, apparently permanently—the feather bed. These square puffs, filled with feathers and slipped into washable linen casings like pillows, are used instead of blankets on the majority of beds. In the best hotels and private homes they are as light as the name implies, in pensions they have frequently become heavy with successive re-coverings and flat with too vigorous pommellings. And in every case, being square and about five feet, they are too short to cover the feet and the shoulders at the same time and too narrow to tuck in at the sides. Furthermore, those which are used in August are precisely the same as those used in December. Since such a puff unites the services of both sheet and blanket, one must either use it *in toto* or discard it *in toto* and lie without benefit of covering. It is singular, in a country where every egg is carefully graded, and where even the groceries are so meticulously classified that one buys milk at one shop and bread at another, that the whole subject of bed-clothing should be lumped in a five-foot feather puff to serve all seasons and all thermal idiosyncrasies. Hans Andersen's Princess who could not sleep with half a dozen feather beds under her was in no worse fix than anyone—not Danish-born—with one such feather bed over him. The only possible answer to the conundrum is that the Danes like five-foot feather puffs.

In the castles and manor-houses of Fünen hang the oil portraits, stand the marble busts, of their founders—ancestors of the present owners. In farmhouses and cottages the names and legends of the great-, the great-great-, the great-great-great-grandparents are handed down by word of mouth. Inevitably, in some of the mansions, the less distinguished portraits find their way to oblivion, and even substantial statues may somehow (and perhaps fortunately) disappear. In the course of centuries the spoken word may be unspoken, or unheard, even around the faithfullest of family hearths. It is impossible for each crowding generation to be remembered in perpetuity. Even in Denmark, where there is such continuity of life, and such reverence for the past, the past recedes. The successive inheritors—and their brides—alter the house, re-allocate the fields, introduce modernity to the stable and dwelling. Those who have gone before become particles of the ether, as the earth ploughed for the thousandth springtime—replanted and reharvested—becomes the soil, the very substance of the country. But the soil of Fünen brings forth richer crops today than it did a thousand years ago. And although the faces of those who once owned it and cultivated it may disappear and even their names be lost, what they contributed in character and deed is indelible in the fibre of their inheritors.

PART IV

"... *the Mirror Up to Nature.*"

CHAPTER ONE

BOOKS AND BUSKINS

O UT of the pageant of hardy sensible Danes, whose two-
thousand-year-old vanguard is led by cheerful Vikings
followed by kings of medieval aggressiveness and brought up
to the present day by phalanxes of rational, highly practical
statesmen, engineers, and scientists, emerge the two Danish
figures which are the best known in the world outside of Denmark. Neither of these possesses hardihood or practicality.
They cannot, by any stretch of the imagination, be called
cheerful. They are, it must be confessed, devoid of rationality
and even common sense. And yet the words they spoke—or
wrote—are known to every school child in the civilized world.
Their immortality is due, at least in part, to their complex and
far from happy personalities.

The first of these is tall and shambling, with a face whose
plain features are refined by a delicacy and an innocence that
set it quite apart from most human countenances. Hans Christian Andersen was the most awkward of men and his lack of
physical attractiveness, like his lack of worldly station, was his
constant pain. From his childhood of poverty, through his
morbid school-days, through his pathetically struggling young

manhood, and even through the period of his fame, he was tortured by the consciousness of his limitations and by an obstinate obsession—in spite of them—to force the attention and win the admiration of the wealthy, the distinguished, and the beautiful men and women of the earth.

That these qualities should have developed into a guileless sycophancy, that he should have presented himself upon the doorstep of every famous person in whose vicinity he happened to be, and having presented himself, should have stayed for weeks on end, and after reluctantly leaving should have continued his association by unwearied and apparently endless correspondence, furnishes part of the material in all his biographies, notably the last and most admirable by Signe Toksvig.

This inability to satisfy an obvious vanity, and this craving —not so obvious—for affirmation of his self-confidence, forced him into a world less inexorable than the one into which he had been born: into the world of imagination. But even after he reached that land of porcelain shepherdesses eloping with porcelain chimney-sweeps and mermaids rescuing princes, and nightingales singing to emperors, he saw and touched and described it with a heart-break too deep for tears. The morals of his tales are not didactic. They are gentle assents to resignation. They are wistful anticipations of a happier day tomorrow.

There is no secret about the life, the loves, the longings of Hans Christian Andersen. "Throughout his long literary life," as Edmund Gosse who knew him remarks, he "never scrupled to make the world his confidant, and that with the utmost sincerity." In fact, his autobiography is so crammed with intimate revelations; his diaries and his letters, to say nothing of his books of travel, so impregnated with self-absorption, that they are ultimately a bit fatiguing as he himself must have been, despite the blameless sweetness of his nature and the crystalline perfection of his art.

There is something amusing and also—to anyone who has affectionately studied him—deliciously satisfying in visiting the house where Andersen was born (April 2, 1805). To this building—which originally housed six families and would have been small for one—have been adjoined several others, to accommodate a museum, a library, an enclosed garden, and a replica of his last chambers. Within it is collected the most amazing assortment of personal possessions, of testimonials, of statues and pictures of Andersen, copies of his books translated into Arabic, Greenlandish, and Chinese, the original drawings by Vilhelm Pedersen to illustrate the tales, the original paper silhouettes Andersen himself cut out with scissors —everything that could have fulfilled his most fantastic flights of egotism.

Such a vast collection of documents, such a scrupulous preservation of the worn luggage which accompanied him on those travels which were his delight, of the top hat which was his badge of ultimate social arrival, of the screens which he made from magazine and newspaper clippings illustrating his own triumphs, of the ten thousand scraps of writing, letters, cards! The flowers he pressed at Paestum are placed beside the very paragraph in his autobiography in which he mentions having received such flowers from a blind girl there. All this assortment of odds and ends may seem disproportionate. It is explained when we remember that "the passion for hoarding up little treasures of every kind—pebbles that friends had picked up, leaves that had been plucked on a certain day, odd mementoes of travel and incident—was always strongly developed in Andersen. He hated to destroy anything, and he dragged about with him, from one lodging to another, a constantly increasing store of what irritable friends were apt to consider rubbish."

No, the multiplicity of these mementoes, their meticulous documentation, the fact that a curator and attendants devote their lives to guarding and displaying them—these things while astonishing are not disproportionate. Hans Christian Andersen was a genius. The word is used soberly. His fairy stories have been translated into thirty-five languages and their sales are superseded by only one other book in the world —the Bible! During the year, forty thousand people come from immense distances to see the house in Odense where he was born. A group of cattle farmers from Lithuania coming to the fair at Odense refused to go to the fair grounds until they had seen Hans Christian Andersen's house. Old ladies from America, children from England, and Rajahs from India flock hither—each one impelled by some childhood memory which has deepened in poignancy with the years. If every word about Andersen should be obliterated, if every memento of him should be destroyed, if his name should be blotted out, those stories which are read by children in Japan and Africa and Arabia, in Chicago and Siberia and Siam—and without doubt would be pored over in Mars if they could be sent there—would achieve a new immortality with every new generation of children. They are unique and they are invaluable and they are Denmark's chief contribution to the literature of the world. Therefore, anything pertaining to their creator has value.

While Andersen's contribution to letters is associated—and

properly—with his fairy-tales, he wrote widely along other lines: travel books, essays, poems, sketches, romances, and plays. This last is the most significant, for Andersen's artistic passion from the time he was a small child and built his own marionette theatre and made the costumes for his tiny puppets was the theatre. He wanted to be an actor and he besieged managers, he hung around stage doors, he importuned playwrights. He cringed under the ridicule directed at his homely face and ungainly body and suffered atrociously with every rebuff. But he persisted, not only in trying to act but in writing plays. And a number of his romantic dramas and fairy comedies were successful at the Royal and at the Casino Theatres in Copenhagen. If his reputation in another field had not been so immense, his smaller one as a playwright would be better known. But although even trifling successes elated him wildly, he did not cease to grieve over his disappointments. He never forgot his longing to be an actor and it is extremely interesting to study, in his later statues, the mobile irregular features and recognize, according to the standards of today and possibly because of their resemblance to George Arliss, their histrionic cast. The fairy-tale, which is the tiny reflection of another universe; the theatre, which ". . . holds the mirror up to Nature"—it was inevitable that a spirit and mentality like Andersen's should have sought expression in these worlds which symbolize rather than embody the actualities of life.

And one is tempted to pursue the analogy by coming to that other immortal Dane who is known wherever Shakespeare is read and whose portrayal seems to be the ambition of every actor who treads the boards.

Whether Hamlet was an actual Prince of Denmark or, as the latest interpretation of the oldest myths has it, "a little more than kin" to Hörder, the god of darkness, who slew Balder, the god of light, or whether he was a legendary figure first mentioned in the thirteenth century by Saxo Grammaticus in his *Historia Danica*, seems likely to remain a matter of speculation.

The Hamlet garbed in inky black who, beside the reopened grave, apostrophizes the skull and, with each generation of actors, queries to each generation of playgoers the advisability of "to be or not to be," is endowed with higher immortality than any flesh and blood princeling or shadowy half-god.

That an Englishman named Will came to Denmark and stayed for a while in the Carmelite Monastery of St. Mary's in Helsingör, and afterward wrote a play about the place he called Elsinore and a prince he called Hamlet—while we are indebted to this rumour for a lively romance by the Danish novelist Sophus Bauditz, it has never received much support from Shakespearian commentators. In the last analysis it is of no more importance than whether it was Bacon who wrote the plays of Shakespeare.

The pale scholar we all know, because we have seen him behind the footlights (although at different times he wore different features and spoke in various accents), is the one true Hamlet—the Hamlet of our imaginations as he was the Hamlet of Shakespeare's genius. It is because of this romantic young man, who embodies all melancholy and impotent despair, not because of Saxo or Balder or Bacon that we—along with the hundred thousand others who yearly make the pilgrimage—travel the twenty-five miles from Copenhagen to Helsingör and to Kronborg Castle with its copper-green towers, its moat and swans, and at its feet the narrowest part of the narrow Sound that lies between Denmark and Sweden.

A poet whose name we are not sure of wrote about people who may never have been born and because of this we find our way to the long Knights' Hall with its black-and-white marble floor which was the stage of a play within a play: to the Queen's Closet once hung with arras and to those battlements upon which

> *"The majesty of buried Denmark*
> *Did sometimes march."*

Perhaps Polonius never hid behind that arras. Perhaps the ghost of the murdered king never walked upon this battlement or those cannon "re-spoke earthly thunder." Perhaps Ophelia did not float with her garlands of nettles and daisies upon yonder weeping brook. It makes no difference. These things not only existed but still exist for that world where Shakespeare so familiarly walked and to which Hans Christian Andersen so wistfully craved admission. . . . "There needs no ghost, my lord, come from the grave to tell us this." . . .

Everything about the theatre is popular in Denmark. Tragedies, comedies, operas, and vaudeville are patronized by a wide and enthusiastic public, and it is appropriate that the Royal Theatre (rebuilt in its present form in 1874 and subsidized by the State) should occupy a conspicuous place in Kongens Nytorv. That no supreme native genius, either as playwright or player, has yet been associated with it, may be due in part to the character of a race more temperate than temperamental, and in part to the smallness of the country and its intimate proximity to the Continent.

The best of the Danish dramatists have possessed either

European blood or European tradition, and the Danish drama had its inception when the Catholic clergy of the Middle Ages imported mystery, miracle, and morality plays from the South. It proceeded from them to the first Danish performances which were cautiously couched in Latin and then to the era when vagabond troupes from Germany and England and strolling players from Holland and France introduced foreign repertoires.

Ludvig Holberg (1684–1754), whose statue with its clever humorous face and fashionable costume sits at the entrance to the Royal Theatre, was the first to hope—and work for—drama which would be truly Danish. Holberg's thirty-one comedies were enormously successful. They are still given and still read, and Marstrand's diverting illustrations of them hang in the State Museum. But although they wittily ridicule snobbery for things foreign, it cannot be denied that the cultivated Holberg, for all his determination to be patriotic, was too closely akin to Molière to produce autochthonous drama. The second classic Danish playwright, Adam Gottlob Oehlenschläger (1779–1850), whose statue balances that of Holberg on the other side of the entrance, although he injected a fresh lyrical feeling into antique Danish allegories, and was a force for over a century in the theatre, was of Teutonic descent with a German and not Danish romanticism of mind.

Since these two who were the first and most famous, numbers of literary men—including Johannes V. Jensen, the most important and original writer in Denmark today—have tried their hand at plays. The lyrical comedies of Drachmann, the problem plays of Ibsen, Edvard Brandes, and others, the satires of Esmann and Wied have been followed by hosts of clever comedy, farce, and vaudeville writers who have enter-

tained pleasure-loving audiences. So even if the Danish theatre has not been particularly important outside of Denmark,
it has been lively and intelligent and modern enough both in
subject matter and scenic effects, and it evinces respect for its
history by its Theatre Museum.

This Museum is in what was once the Royal Theatre and
part of the Christianborg Palace, and the Royal Box, hung
with crimson velvet, and Christian VIII's picture on the wall
are still preserved.

It is small but it manages two balconies and is opulently
decorated in terra-cotta and gold. The floor of the exag-
geratedly deep stage inclines, in the old-fashioned manner,
with the same sharp angle as the floor of the pit, and a reed
organ indicates the orchestra.

No plays are given now in this bijou playhouse, which is
hunted out by all visitors interested in the stage. For here are
the busts and portraits of famous players, and programmes
and play bills from 1773. These are far from provincial, for
the Danish stage has never broken its tradition of hospitality
to foreigners. The Museum has mementoes of Jenny Lind,
who sang here (Hans Christian Andersen was in love with her),
of Strindberg, Björnson, and Ibsen, who had Danish blood in
his veins and naturally turned to Copenhagen for a welcome.
He received a handsome one. All his plays were not only
given for the first time in the Royal Theatre but here were
conceived, under Ibsen's own direction, the stage settings
which have been used ever since in theatres all over the world.

Danish plays may not be well known abroad, but Danish
tragedians and comedians have taken curtain calls behind
footlights far from home. The first foreigner ever to play at
the Comédie Française was Poul Reunert as Tartuffe. The

legitimate English-speaking stage has been honoured by Eva Le Gallienne, who is half Danish, and Hollywood has discovered Johannes Poulsen and Jean Hersholt.

A plain white-painted desk in the corridor of the Museum is of special interest, for upon it Karl Mantzius wrote those five scholarly volumes on *A History of Theatrical Art,* which are the dictionary, encyclopædia, and Bible of all students of the theatre everywhere. Mantzius is so well known as the author of this prodigious work that many visitors to the Theatre Museum are surprised to see beside the desk the statue of him in one of his favourite roles and also his old make-up box and realize that the scholar was also an actor and an excellent and versatile one. The desk likewise recalls his distinguished father, Kristian, who played in this small theatre while Karl played at the Royal.

The theatre in Denmark has a not unworthy reputation, and the Museum has its interest. But the ballet in Denmark overleaps such moderation of praise, for it is unqualifiedly excellent and second in brilliance only to that of Russia.

Since the Middle Ages the dance has been popular in Denmark. Five hundred years ago, from king's court to Icelandic farm-stead, people delighted in the "carole"—that circular dance whose measures are carried out with joined hands and singing and which still survives in the Faroe Islands. (The ballad has always been closely associated with the dance, as the Italian word *ballare* suggests.) In the early 1100's every knight had his own dancing grounds as do the Papuan chiefs at the present day. The Church protested against a pastime too dangerously associated with Beltane fires—and protested in vain. Even Bishop Absalon was powerless to stop the "light heeled frolic" of the monks of Eskilö. In 1425 the Church

Graduation from the University in Copenhagen is celebrated with processions and parades.

ALLEGHENY COLLEGE LIBRARY

Despite laws of disentailment and heavy taxes, castles are still plentiful as plums in a plum cake.

ALLEGHENY COLLEGE LIBRARY

The cottage in Falster where Marie Grubbe lived as a ferryman's
wife is still occupied.

ALLEGHENY COLLEGE LIBRARY

Denmark pays special attention to its children, but not all baby-
tending is institutionalized.

ALLEGHENY COLLEGE LIBRARY

forbade "heathen songs and dances on the feast of St. John." And nevertheless the dance went on and the churchyard remained a popular place for it. The leader sang the ballad proper, the others coming in with the refrain.

Upon such congenial soil it is not strange that the ballet should have developed, flourished, and flowered, or that the Theatre Museum should have its ballet room. It is presided over by the master Galeotti and he is surrounded by ladies whose plump curves would put them out of business today. Possibly our ideas need correction, for as Isak Dinesen observes in "The Poet," "Lightness that is not only the negation of weight, but which actually seems to carry upward and make for flight is rarely found in thin dancers—as if the matter itself had here become lighter than air, so that the more there is of it, the better it works." At all events, Galeotti with the aid of these tightly corseted damsels worked out an art of which a contemporary critic said: "It is not the senses alone which man gratifies by his situations and tableaux, his action and his pantomime, but the soul as well." Galeotti lived to be nearly ninety and reigned over the Danish ballet for forty years. After him came Cetti with his tight-rope walking pantomimes and Casorti, whose dainty mimicries still grace the Peacock Theatre in Tivoli. But it was Auguste Bournonville—whose French father came as a solo dancer to Copenhagen in 1792—who was the worthy successor of the great Galeotti. "No one," says Edmund Gosse, "desirous of comprehending the spirit of Denmark in the middle of the nineteenth century with its peculiar grace, sentimentality, and irony, can avoid a study of the ballets of Bournonville," and adds: "This poet, to whom the gift of words was denied, retained instead the most divine faculty for devising intricate and exquisite cadences of movement, and for framing stories of a dramatic kind, in which all the action is performed in dumb show and consists of a succession of mingled tableaux and dances."

The Danes not only enjoy watching the ballet, but are irresistibly impelled—at the drawing of a bow—to dance themselves. When a fashionable hotel in Aalborg started the custom of having the orchestra appear once a week in folk costume and giving a programme of folk dances, the fun was not long confined to the orchestra. The diners need no folk costumes and apparently no lessons in folk dancing. They tread with gusto the complicated measures of old-fashioned square and round and processional dances and end up with mazurkas and polkas which would do credit to professionals and with waltzes which testify that in Denmark the Merry Widow is as merry as ever she was.

The literature of any country must be translated before it can be enjoyed by the rank and file of foreigners, and that which is most precious and most characteristic—its poetry—slips out of the net of the closest of translators. The Danes are great readers: Maurice Francis Egan, who was American Minister to Denmark (1907–1918), considered the Gyldendalske Book Concern "the most important publication house in Scandinavia." But one who does not read Danish will get a hardly more correct or comprehensive idea of Danish literature from the few available translations than the idea of English and American letters formed by those Danes whose reading is limited to Ethel M. Dell and Sinclair Lewis. In this connexion it might be mentioned that there are still many of Hans Christian Andersen's tales which have never appeared in English, and others which have reached their English editions only via translation from the German.

It is fortunate that the art which Denmark has preserved and perfected—the ballet—needs no translation. When Adeline Genée curvetted through the dashing leaps of her hunting dance, when she pirouetted through her "Dream of Butterflies and Roses" like a rosebud twirled between thumb and finger, few of her tempestuously applauding public remembered—if they ever knew—that this frolicking, joyous ballerina was born Petersen in Jutland and was carrying on the tradition of her family and her race.

Since the end of imperial patronage in Russia, there has been no place in Europe with as large and excellent *corps de ballet* as the Royal Theatre in Copenhagen. It maintains its own school into which pupils are admitted at four years of age and frequently remain the rest of their lives. At many performances at the Royal Theatre one sees a group of tiny children in the topmost box—like cherubs poised in the clouds —intently studying every motion, gesture, and step of that complex statement of the dance which, when it passed from the amateur to the artist, from the court to the theatre, passed also from an elegant accomplishment to a serious science.

Any dramatic production at the Royal Theatre is sure to be good, but the ballet is certain to be superb.

Fortunately for foreigners to whom intimacy with the Danish spirit through literature is denied, the ballets which Bournonville created upon Danish motives, and upon which the present-day repertoires still partially rest, interpret the balance, humour, good spirits, and passion for perfection of the racial rhythm. An art as fugitive as breath and a science as precise as mathematics, the ballet holds its small clear mirror up to Nature.

CHAPTER TWO

THE KINGDOM OF THE EYE

DOWN in the south of Fünen lies the town of Faaborg, dainty as old lace, fresh as a rosebud on a venerable rose-bush. It is complete with city gate and bell tower, with ancient timbered houses and shops newly whitewashed, with swinging street signs and alleys leading into courtyard gardens or opening to the sea. Around it to the west the hills of Svanninge rollick demurely away toward the Castle of Brahetrolleborg; around it, to the south and east, dance the waters of the Little Belt. Surely there is no more winsome town in all the world than Faaborg.

And directly one enters it, as if to defy the sentimentality of mere prettiness, one is confronted—indeed, abruptly halted —by the monumental sculpture of Kaj Nielsen depicting the Ymer Well. Its elemental choice of subject and its block effect, unmarred by any break or piercing through in the heavy yet plastic mass, are supremely characteristic of this sculptor in whose too early death Denmark feels she has lost one of the masters of modern times. For a country which, in the field of the fine arts, as Emil Hannover admits, has "always been as lacking in genius as it has been rich in first-rate talent," this is a loss indeed. Kaj Nielsen lived long enough, however, and his creative and physical powers were great enough for him to have left many heroic works through whose marble stone and lesser materials surges delight in mighty lines and fecund forms, and smaller ones in which his dexterity and roguishness find happy expression. Perhaps he was more successful in these latter: the Museum at Faaborg is almost overpowered by his enormous granite statue of the founder.

For this diminutive town of Faaborg contains a new building even more remarkable than any of the old—a museum in which is collected representative examples from the beginning of the twentieth century when a group called the Fünen painters opened up a new era in Danish art. If Denmark has not produced immortal sculptors and painters, she has cherished whatever gifted ones she had, classifying them as realists, colourists, illustrators, landscape and figure painters, nationalists, and so forth, and her museums are arranged with such intelligence and taste that they are thoroughly informative and enjoyable. The Museum of Faaborg naturally cannot be compared in size or richness to the great ones in Copenhagen. Its significance lies in the fact that such an institution exists in such a place. Respect for and interest in its own æsthetic accomplishments is characteristic of the small country whose only world-famous sculptor was Thorvaldsen (unless we include Gutzon Borglum, both of whose parents were Danes).

Thorvaldsen (1770–1844) was the son of an Icelandic wood carver and a Jutland girl. He was born in Copenhagen, and in Copenhagen one of the most striking buildings in one of the most central sites is the Museum which not only bears his name but whose vestibules, corridors, lower and upper rooms, courtyard, and even basement contain his works and his only, his collections of coins, bronzes, and paintings, portraits of him and some of his personal possessions.

The building is two stories high, in the style of an Etruscan tomb, with the sculptor's grave in the centre of the courtyard. Its exterior walls are enlivened by *sgraffito* decorations representing scenes in his life—these are by Sonne—and the principal façade is surmounted by the bronze Victory in her Chariot completed by Bissen from the master's design. Within this unique memorial are statues by the score, busts by the dozen, bas-reliefs by the acre, plaster and marble by the ton. There are sketches, models, reproductions of work whose originals are elsewhere—literally several thousand figures.

A foreigner from any country surveys this multitude of gods, heroes, cupids, Christian saints, portrait busts, shepherd boys, mythological animals, muses, graces, genii, with a shock not of novelty but of familiarity. Those bas-reliefs of Morning and Night hung in plaster replicas upon our nursery walls; that Jason with the Golden Fleece stood in our school auditorium; the Lion of Lucerne adorned the mantelpiece in our grandparents'—nearly everyone's grandparents'—home. It is as difficult to appraise the artistic worth of objects with such association as to analyse dispassionately the literary merits of *David Copperfield!*

During his long, happy, and productive life—whose dates of birth and death exactly confine the period of the classical revival, and nearly forty years of which were spent in Italy— his admiring contemporaries and his proud countrymen compared Thorvaldsen to Phidias and Praxiteles. They acclaimed in him the rebirth of Hellenism and never suspected that this "distinctively cool, clear, pure, and calm reproduction of

antiquity was really nothing more than a reflection of Greece
on a Northern artist's soul."

But if his contemporaries gave him too exalted a rank, the
modern fashion of dismissing him as an imitator and his works
as lifeless stereotypes is also in need of correction. Balance and
unity are enduring virtues. And that unchanging beatific peace
which characterized Thorvaldsen's own spirit, that shines forth
from Eckersberg's justly famous portrait of him, that serenity
which informed everything he moulded, still has power to
charm. We need not accept the perfervid eulogies. We may
even be permitted to smile at the indulgent admission that if
the Lion of Lucerne has serious faults these arise "mainly
from the fact that the sculptor had never seen a lion."

Emil Hannover's words will probably remain for a long
time as the most constructive and judicious estimate of this
beloved man and artist. "Though Thorvaldsen was entirely
devoid of higher education and therefore disdained all the
requirements which the æsthetes of the time exacted of the
educated artist, he none the less appeared to his contemporaries to be the fulfilment of their æsthetic theory; if all the
dreams and expectations of the period were fulfilled in him,
it was primarily because what they had been dreaming of and
longing for with glowing passion was not, fundamentally, the
rebirth of ancient art or of the classical conception of the human figure, but the rebirth of the actual human spirit of
antiquity. Something of the most primitive and happy quality
of that spirit, something of its purity and serenity, something
of all that which in Europe generally life had almost poi-
soned and erudition had almost corrupted, was brought on
the world's artistic stage about 1800 by this youth who had

neither read nor lived. It was no mere accident that he came from an obscure little country. Only from an out-of-the-way corner of the world, where life had stood still for centuries, where the primitive spirit of humanity had been preserved, could an artist have come with such pristine simplicity as his. Appearing at the opportune and decisive moment, this was Denmark's most significant contribution to the culture of the world."

If there are only two Danish sculptors who can be said to have reached world-wide recognition, Danish painters cannot claim even that distinction. There is no Titian or Rembrandt or Velazquez, there is no Cézanne, there is not even a Sir Joshua Reynolds. Nevertheless, there have been plenty of painters in Denmark and there are plenty of their pictures displayed advantageously for them and conveniently for the spectator. An unprejudiced examination of these from the very first—the Academy of Fine Arts was not founded until 1784 and Abildgaard is usually considered the first genuinely Danish painter—to the moderns who are so interestingly represented in the Faaborg Museum, indicates that while none have reached the supreme heights of genius, the average of talent and taste and intelligenec is entirely creditable. Denmark has no mountains, abysses, raging rivers, or hideous slums, and the Danish character is more notable for moderation than inspired madness. Those to whom these unpretentious qualities are not unpleasing will find them agreeably reflected on the walls of the various museums.

The early painters were influenced by Europe. Jens Juel was a follower of Rousseau. Fritzsch learned his brush work from the seventeenth-century French and Dutch flower specialists. Eckersberg was quickened by Italy before he discovered his native sea. Those who followed gradually discovered the Danish scene and interpreted it with varying degrees of fidelity and feeling.

There are, of course, the large historical canvases—such as the popular one by Carl Bloch showing King Christian II in his prison at Sönderborg, and those by Zahrtmann depicting Leonora Christina as an old woman. There are the narrative studies of rural life by Dalsgaard and the excellent fun-making illustrations of Marstrand. But nearer and dearer are the loving studies of the peasants of Amager by Exner and of the fishermen of Fanö, the winter scenes of Johan Rohde, the chestnut trees and a farmhouse by Viggo Pedersen, the sunflowers of Thorvald Niss, Vermehren's Shepherd on the Heath, and Johannes Larsen's wild ducks.

These pictures are not epoch-making in the long history of the art of the world, but they will hold a certain appeal while purple heather clings to the moors, and clouds and storms and sunshine pass over the gentle surface of the Danish countryside. As long as young lambs browse among barrows older than historic time, as long as horses graze on the wind-swept fields of Saltholm and cows gather in the late afternoon in milking places under the sky; as long as fishermen look out over the sands of the Skaw and the summer night holds the hushed lake in darkening trance, the pictures of Lundbye, Philipsen, Kröyer, and Köbke will be loved by Danes.

The quiet, plain interiors of Vilhelm Hammershöi, grey upon grey, with a single dark feminine form seated with its back to us—these subdued and sensitive studies have won admirers far beyond Denmark—and Joakim Skovgaard's tremendous frescoes which decorate Viborg Cathedral have received—in fact, demanded—more than local attention. The modernists cannot be accused of placidity. Beginning with Edvard Weie, to whom the State Museum devotes an entire wall, and continuing through the Cubism of Vilhelm Lundström and the "music and structure" of Harald Giersing, they find hospitality not only in the museums but in art shops and private homes—and in the storage of their own studios. Their swirls and streaks and splashes of "pure colour" and their untrammelled interpretation of form and design are as difficult for the layman to understand as their names are for the foreigner to remember. But at all events, they indicate that even in cautious and rational Denmark, youth is experimenting.

The Museum at Faaborg is indicative of Denmark's scholarly-minded attitude toward whatever achievement in the fine arts she may claim, and another example of this is the Music History Museum—connected with the Museum of Applied Arts (Kunstindustrimuseet)—in Copenhagen.

Here among a varied collection of exotic curios—African tomtoms, deep-toned gongs from China, Norwegian violins and lyres carved and inlaid, Italian harpsichords, their slim sides ivoried with age and delicately decorated with scrolls and arabesques—are replicas of that tremendous wind instrument, the lur, which, curved like the horn of an animal, was carried—always in pairs—in prehistoric ceremonial processions. The first of these lurs, which date from the Bronze Age, was found in a bog near Copenhagen (1797), the bog not only having concealed it for centuries but actually preserved it, so that it is still possible for it to utter its full and pompous tones. This primitive trumpet, so distinctively Danish (similar forms have been unearthed only in South Sweden and Norway and North Germany and, oddly, in Ireland), has been effectively incorporated in the Lur Blowers Column near the

City Hall, and has given its name as a trade mark to various
dairy products, although its occasional appearance today is
more an historical than a musical accompaniment to some
national festival.

Among the rich relics of other days—old gold-and-white music boxes playing Haydn, Renaissance pochettes, little great-
grandmothers of the violin, ivory and wood "recorders" such
as Rosencrantz and Guildenstern held before Hamlet—are
mementoes of those few composers whom Denmark can claim
as her own. If little known beyond the land of their birth,
they are assured of local immortality. Here is the ebony and
silver baton with which Niels Gade conducted—Niels Gade,
who has left his record in England where, at the Birming-
ham festival (1876), he conducted his Zion and The Crusaders.
His Ossian Overture and Symphony in C minor were admired
by Mendelssohn and Schumann, and he became, after the
death of the former, the conductor of the Leipzig Gewand-
haus. So reposeful and well proportioned are Gade's themes,
so suave his instrumentation, that he holds a rightful niche
in the gallery of European composers. So, likewise, does Carl
Nielsen, the strongest and most original of Danish musicians,
whose instrumental works are known in musical circles everywhere and whose songs and ballads are perennially popular
throughout Denmark. The Music History Museum, preserving his square piano—of Danish manufacture—and many pictures of him and letters by him, keeps his memory green.
There is another name which has a familiar look to those
visitors who "took music lessons" in those far-away days before gramophones and radios did it all—Kuhlau, whose student pieces were dutifully thrummed out during practice
hours from Boston to Buenos Aires. Here in a mahogany case

is the hammer clavier with four octaves upon which he composed those well-known sonatas.

Hartmann, who is credited with having influenced Grieg; Buxtehude, to whom Sebastian Bach came for instruction; Weyse, known to students of musical history—of all these the Museum piously preserves memorabilia.

The composers of Denmark, like its painters, reflect the mild nuances and harmonious colouring of their environment, expressing these things with a refined symmetry and a spontaneity which makes no pretence to high passion.

Although here, as elsewhere, folk songs and ballads, legends, and music chants have existed since earliest times—probably before the church music imported from the South—and although these tunes with their robust balance and refreshing intervals have been utilized by native composers, Danish music properly can be said to have existed only since about 1800. And although the Royal Theatre has seen many operas written, conducted, sung, and acted by Danes, the native taste has always been more inclined to lighter song sketches and vaudeville and, of course, the incomparable ballet.

One reason why the fine arts of Denmark interest the foreigner beyond what their actual merits might suggest is that the museums are so remarkably well arranged.

If one wants a complete survey of Danish painters he can find it in the State Museum. If he is especially interested in the nineteenth century there is the Hirschsprung Collection. And the Glyptotek, whose two great sections are united by a crystal dome forming a winter garden, presents its vast assemblage of antique and modern, foreign and native sculpture and painting with a graceful hospitality which lifts it out of the usual pattern of museums.

Here is not only the most splendid collection of antique portraits in marble in the world, but the largest collection of French sculpture outside of France. Here are not only van Goghs and Millets and Cézannes and Corots, but the Danish canvases of Lundbye, Kröyer, and Skovgaard. As for Gauguin —a whole long room is given over to his hot, velvety yellows and reds and purples. For Gauguin, it may be remembered, married a Danish wife and when he left her he also left (besides a number of French Impressionists he had been shrewd enough to collect) a son, Jean Gauguin, who does not depend upon his father's notoriety to hold his own place as a sculptor.

The Glyptotek is extraordinarily enjoyable, with its summer gardens outside and its winter garden inside, with its courtyards and corridors and marble-floored Emperors Hall. Etruscan maidens with enigmatic lips look down on Danish school children being shepherded past. The lions of ancient Greece roar from limestone friezes and the sunshine which falls on Rodin's Les Océanides touches also the full maternal limbs of Kaj Nielsen's Water Mother. Examples of the best from ages that are past, and honour for the best from the age that is here—the Glyptotek combines these with felicity and taste.

The Glyptotek originated in the private art collection of a wealthy brewer and its maintenance and purchases are made possible by money which he left for that purpose. There is nothing unusual in a public-spirited rich man. There is nothing unusual in a legacy left to a worthy institution. But there is something not only unusual but unique about the Carlsberg Foundation.

The great brewery of Carlsberg, which caps a million and a half bottles of beer a day, gives not a part but its entire profits to art and science! Furthermore, the brewery which was built privately is not owned by an individual. It has no stockholders and its directors are members of the Royal Danish Academy of Science and Letters—triumphant refutation of the slander against the impracticality of professors. It is a huge business, paying as much as seventeen million kroner a year in taxes. A staff of men is kept constantly busy conducting scientists, visiting brewers, and tourists over the enormous plant—and, incidentally, seating them in handsome dining-rooms when the sightseeing is over, and offering them hospitality. It ships its beer and mineral waters all over the world. And as the beer flows out and the money flows in, this latter is diverted directly and in its entirety to the intellectual and idealistic furtherance of public good.

The founder of the Carlsberg Brewery, J. C. Jacobsen, was a master brewer who believed that good beer is the best weapon against distilled liquors. In his laboratory Professor Emil Chr. Hansen discovered the pure yeast cell which made possible a certain and stable process of fermentation. With the great fortune J. C. Jacobsen amassed he established a Foundation which had three purposes. First, a laboratory for experimenting in brewing and also along other branches, with the explicit provision that "no results whatever of the work of the Institute whether of a theoretical or practical nature shall be kept secret." Second, the support of science in general and various branches of research. Third, the restoration of the vast Frederiksborg Castle which had been burned in 1859. This did not confine itself to rebuilding, in the most sumptuous manner, the actual walls and towers, but extended to furnishings and such treasures that the Castle is now properly called the Frederiksborg National History Museum.

While these were the primary benefactions of J. C. Jacobsen, statues without number, the greenhouses of the Botanical Gardens, the lobby of the Royal Theatre, and countless other embellishments of the city owe their existence to him.

His son, Carl Jacobsen, was also a brewer and established his own successful brewery and followed his father's example in devoting the profits from it to a Foundation. But since the son was primarily interested in art and in educating the taste of his countrymen, the New Carlsberg Foundation began with the Glyptotek.

Today the two breweries are merged in one tremendous organization, but the two Foundations—although closely associated and usually spoken of as one—are separate institutions. The profits from the brewery are almost equally divided between them. Munificent, intelligently administered, with an enlightened concept of the needs of science and art, the Carlsberg Foundation has done more for Denmark than the gifts of any king. The Academy of Science, the Glyptotek, the Biological Institute (founded by the Carlsberg Foundation in conjunction with the Rockefeller Foundation), museums in the provinces, restoration of ancient buildings and decoration of new, the publication of books dealing with the fine arts, travelling grants to artists, and support of the applied arts—every sort of scientific and artistic endeavour is stimulated, nurtured, and advanced by it. It is not possible to state the amount of the capital of the Foundation; its yearly income surpasses a million and a half kroner. One of the lesser but most imaginative bequests was that of J. C. Jacobsen, who left his handsome villa, with sufficient endowment for its upkeep, as a free and honorary residence for life for any man or woman —selected by the directors of the Foundation—outstanding in

science, literature, the fine arts, or any other noteworthy line
of endeavour. At present this mansion, with its gardens, is occupied by Professor Niels Bohr, the founder of the modern
atomic theory.

The Carlsberg is the greatest of the Danish Foundations,
but it is not the oldest.

As long ago as 1811 the Hielmstierne-Rosencrone was established, from which ten to twenty thousand kroner are annually distributed chiefly for the support of the study of Danish
history. And as recently as 1931, Tuborg—another enormous
brewery in Copenhagen capping two million bottles of beer
and mineral water yearly—established a Foundation "to pro-
mote objects of benefit to society and especially to support
Danish trade and industrial life," and has extended its patronage to various scientific institutions as well. The Rask-Oersted
Foundation which was established by an Act of Parliament
(1919) endows Danish contributions to international research,
supports periodicals of an international character directed by
Danes or other Scandinavians, lends its aid to international
scientific meetings, assists foreign scientists in Denmark and
Danish scientists abroad, enables Danish scientists to publish
their works in a world language, and has even gone so far in
its international zeal as to present the League of Nations with
fifty thousand kroner.

Wherever one turns in Denmark there are evidences of
similar generosity. Besides Otto Monsted's Foundation—with
a capital of twenty-three million kroner and primarily con-
cerned with commercial and industrial advancement—there
are over a score of others testifying that for many generations
Denmark has believed that "now is the time for all good men
to come to the aid of the party."

It is significant that in a country where everyone contributes in taxes to an extensive programme of social and scientific betterment there should be so many voluntary and lavish endowments by individuals, and that they should encircle such a wide and impersonal range of objectives.

It is no mere chance that the list of Danish men of science should be remarkable.

In making such a list, we should realize that few things are harder than to estimate justly the value of a scientific discovery. That value lies in the consequences, and the account is never closed; each generation makes a fresh estimate. There are many names now distinguished to which our successors will accord only a minor eminence, while other men, now hardly noticed, will be seen to have been of the true immortal breed. However, there are a few names whose place in the history of science is secure. If a country can produce men of this lustre the lesser luminaries may be taken for granted.

Tycho Brahe (1546–1601) was by common consent the greatest of all practical astronomers. Astronomical instruments of his day were crude affairs, but the accuracy of Tycho Brahe's long series of observations was not surpassed for nearly a century. Particularly is this true of his observations of the planets. At his death he left his papers to his pupil, Kepler, and it was by the use of these that Kepler discovered his laws of planetary motion. Newton, in turn, based his theory of gravitation on the work of Kepler. Hypothetical history is an uncertain science, but it is not unreasonable to believe that without Brahe's incomparable skill and patience the world might well have waited another century to solve the riddle of the solar system.

Olaus (Ole) Römer (1644–1710) was another astronomer. While on a visit to the Paris Observatory he made some observations on the satellites of Jupiter. He noticed that the periods of revolution were irregular, being shorter when the earth approached the planet than when it was receding. This he was able to account for by supposing that light did not travel instantaneously, but took some time to cross the intervening space. This conclusion was so at variance with the accepted belief of the followers of Descartes that his ideas at first made little headway. Today we look on Römer's discovery as the initial step toward our understanding of the nature of light.

To Hans Christian Oersted (1777–1851) belongs the glory of having first discovered the effect of an electric current on a magnet. He not only discovered it, but he formed a correct view of the real nature of the phenomenon. His account of his discovery, published in 1820, marks the beginning of our knowledge of electro-magnetism. "Behold how great a matter a little fire kindleth"; the wildest imagination could not have pictured the myriad ways in which the motion of Oersted's compass-needle is exemplified in our modern electric motors. Recently, an international electrical congress has preserved Oersted's name for future generations by attaching it, like the names of Volta, Ampère, and Ohm, to one of the electrical units.

One other name must be emphasized—that of a living man. It is not often that we can anticipate the verdict of history, but the work of Niels Bohr on the constitution of atoms has opened up already such vistas into the unknown that his permanent place in the company of pathfinders is assured.

These are tremendous names, and they deal with matters beyond the comprehension—or vocabulary—of the layman. Any country might justly be proud of them.

And any country, too, might be proud of the attitude toward knowledge and the respect for things artistic or archæological which are exemplified in the following humble incident.

In the Folk Museum—not the Art Museum—at Faaborg there is the trunk of an oak hollowed out and roughly shaped. A few months ago a fisherman, chancing upon it, recognized it for what it might be, salvaged it, and carried it to the Museum. It is a Viking coffin and for years—who can say how many hundred—had been drifting—who can say where?

"Art is a serious thing in Denmark and often it is taken too seriously by people of no talent," observed a former American Minister to Denmark. Mr. Egan's implication might be argued. For only when people of no talent—and perhaps of no importance—take art seriously can the artist live, or those things which genius has wrought under other skies be brought in and appreciated. "At least," as Hamlet says, "I'm sure it may be so in Denmark."

CHAPTER THREE

THE ARTS OF PEACE

DENMARK'S distinction rests upon quality rather than size, and this distinction is reflected in an art which has been associated with her name for many years—those small, choice porcelain figures in which the fancifulness of the subject is perfectly expressed through the taste of the artist and the technique of the craftsman.

Even during the present fashion of eschewing mere ornamentation, these trifles have held their tiny inviolacy. Defying the practicality of the age, they continue to embrace romance. Disregarding economic stress, they embody in their fine clays and glazes the epitome of fragile luxury.

Denmark, the kingdom of reason, is populated with fauns with cloven feet sporting with maidens clad in garlands of rosebuds, and emperors naked but for a sceptre and a shirt; with sea horses and mermen and mermaids and four-inch snow-white crocodiles and elephants. It takes forty days for a skilled brush man—or more often brush woman—to paint the patterns of the fabrics, to colour the infinitesimal nosegays, every petal rolled by hand, every leaf twisted between human fingers, to gild and jewel the ribbons, ear-rings,

buckles, and braids on these statues of exquisite femininity.
And it may take as many as seventy different moulds to shape
them. The more elaborate of these sell for hundreds of dollars. The Princess on the Pea—her ruffled robe and underskirt
in shades of grey, her turban, cuffs, and slippers of rose, a
blue turquoise on her pompadour—draws herself up in be-
witching discomfort high on top of five little feather beds.
Their brocaded covers of purple and blue and rose and grey,
with swinging golden bells on every corner, conceal but cannot disguise the fact that there is a cruel pea at the bottom!
This is a unique piece and whoever has a taste and a place for
it must pay thirty-five hundred kroner and it would not be
dear.

Hans Christian Andersen's heroes and heroines, half spirit
and half sprite, found suitable tangibility in the Royal Copenhagen porcelain just as certain of Thorvaldsen's bas-
reliefs have found theirs in the marmoreal ceramics of Bing
and Gröndahl—the two famous factories of Denmark. But
although this dainty genre has had its specialized artists, its
specialized technicians, and its appreciative purchasers for over
a hundred and fifty years, both factories have extended their
operations to articles of general utility. The traditional white
sail boat on the traditional blue sea is still painted in that most
difficult of techniques—the under-glaze—upon the traditional
vases. But new materials, new glazes, new forms are continually created. The Royal Copenhagen Porcelain Factory turns
out the most modern of faience table services: Jean Gauguin's
fountains—one of which was bought by the French Government for the Tuileries—not only mark a new spirit in ceramics
but have achieved a new and colossal scale.

Denmark would not be Denmark without the blue-and-white table-ware—each line and dot put on by hand—without the sleeping cats which lend themselves so obligingly to the flowing lines of porcelain, quite unlike their angular Egyptian counterparts cast in eternal bronze. But Denmark would not be Denmark if it were not experimenting.

Some of the modern pottery, terra-cotta, and stone-ware is extremely interesting. The fine porcelain clay for the Royal Copenhagen Factory is imported from Germany, the fine pottery clay from England. But these young artists are using native materials. And they are using local models. The subtle statuettes of Gerhard Henning reflect the artificiality of France, and are appropriately set forth in precious porcelain over-glaze; Malinowski's enigmatic semi-Oriental fictilia are in white biscuit. But the rollicking fisherwoman from Hjorth's factory in Bornholm is a Bornholm woman and she is modelled in broad humour out of Bornholm clay. In Jutland, Matilde Nielsen and her daughters are fashioning by hand, without a wheel, pitchers and bowls of the same form and the same finish as those left from the Roman age and found in Pompeii and Herculaneum. These pottery forms of primitive design and surfaces revealing the smoothing of the human hand are frozen during the winter night before they are baked in an earth oven—a return, indeed, to archaic methods! Horn painting has come back into its own, and follows the homely technique. A goose quill is pushed through a cork and the cork is fitted into the end of a cow's horn which holds the paint. The design is scratched with the quill upon the damp clay so that it is simultaneously coloured and indented, giving its unique decoration to tiles and dishes.

All the new forms are not primitive. Nathalie Krebs in her Saxbo stone-ware has achieved, in restrained simplicity of form and in glazes of brown, imperial yellow, lavender, blue, and brick-red, a tranquil and absolute distinction which may be compared to the best of Chinese ceramics of the same type. Neither are all the forms autochthonous. From Andersen Brothers' factory, also in Bornholm, float angels and Madonnas quite Italian in their sentiment.

There has been nothing revolutionary in this admirable progression of the ceramic art. Priceless porcelains and amusing stone-ware express with equal genuineness the Danish spirit of playfulness, the instinct to make beautiful everyday articles of use, and pleasure in interpreting the simple and the familiar. The horn painter decorates a broad-beamed pig, and the most expensive porcelain lends itself to pinafored children and to those domestic animals—the high-bred dogs, the pretty cows, the white ducks and geese which fleck the meadows and the ponds—without which the remembrance of any Danish scene would be incomplete.

The dainty porcelain, the jolly pottery symbolize Danish taste. The silver, serene and solid, symbolizes Danish character. Together they make festive the shop windows and enrich museums and homes.

Danish silver has been handsome and honest for years. Recently it has become fashionable all over the world and most foreigners associate it with the name of Georg Jensen. This is entirely proper, for Georg Jensen was an artist who was fortunate enough to discover the precise medium for his genius, or, rather, from a familiar material to draw out a new and undiscovered æsthetic value.

Before he became a silversmith—although after he had served four years' apprenticeship with a goldsmith—he studied sculpture at the Academy of Arts, and the exhibition of his first large piece—The Harvester—was praised for the purity of its strength and excellence of its composition. He won the Academy's gold medal and the travel legacy which went with it, and set forth to France and Italy. In the museums he studied not only sculpture with an artist's eye but the work of great goldsmiths and silversmiths with a craftsman's eye. When he was thirty-eight he exhibited as a sculptor for the last time, and in a small room with one apprentice he opened his first workshop. A year later his silver was recognized at an exhibition in Hagen, Germany; five years later a gold medal was awarded him at Brussels, and after that he exhibited annually at the Paris Salon. Today his work is not only sold in every country, but it is given a place of honour in the museums of Europe and America.

Like the great craftsmen of the Renaissance, Jensen had tremendous creative energy. For years he not only designed every piece which came from his establishment: he supervised its making, directed the daily work, planned exhibitions, undertook the foreign journeys necessitated by it, and at one exhibition in London displayed nearly seven hundred pieces, most of which were the work of his own hands. Again, like the Renaissance artists, he had a dynamic personality and knew how to choose, train, and inspire his collaborators and assistants, so that when he died at sixty-nine (1935) he left something far more than a factory. He had established a school, with followers, standards, and traditions, and so strong was his impulse and so true were his principles that this has continued to grow after his death.

What Georg Jensen recognized was that silver has a character of its own. It is a heavy material and, therefore, it should not be hammered thin. It is a soft material and, therefore, its forms should be pliant. His training as a sculptor enabled him to give his silver a special plasticity, and by treating the surface with a mallet to remove shininess and then covering it with a thin coating of platinum, he produced articles which are absolutely unmistakable and uncopyable. Whether it is jewellery, table-ware, objects of utility, or pure art, Georg Jensen's silver looks like Georg Jensen's silver and like that of no one else.

From over-ornamentation he worked toward simplification and grew in clarity and repose. His style is classical and at the same time highly modern. Like all great artists, he had his imitators and his detractors, but the fact remains that he may be called the greatest designer of silver since Paul de Lamerie in the eighteenth century.

Georg Jensen was not the sole silversmith of Denmark. There have been skilful Danish metal workers for centuries, and today there are young artists with fresh and modern styles: Frantz Hingelberg's clean forms; Carl Cohr's plated silver and stainless steel, not hand-made but excellent; Just Andersen's patinated bronze and disco metals. The aristocratic elegancies of P. Hertz and P. A. Michelsen, the Court Jeweller, are more popular with certain Copenhageners than the Georg Jensen silver, which they think too massive.

The place to see what is being done in the many fields of the decorative and applied arts is at the Permanent Industrial Exhibition, quite in the centre of the city, open and free at all times, and giving two thousand metres of space to objects made in Denmark. Here the various ceramic factories and silversmiths display their best examples. Here are bronze and pewter and glass and engraved crystal; amber, jewellery, hand-woven textiles and laces. Here are toys and leather-ware and wooden dishes; knitted mittens and caps from the Faroe Islands; ivory, bone, bead-work and feather-work from Greenland. Interest in all handicraft has led to the organization of several societies whose aims are artistic and philanthropic rather than commercial. Thus the Society for the Promotion of Handicrafts (Selskabet til Haandarbejdets Fremme) started in 1928 to prove that Danish women had not lost their skill with needle and loom and also to give those who could not leave home an opportunity to earn money. Old patterns and designs are made available, weaving is taught, and a committee of artists approves every piece before it is displayed for sale. The Carlsberg Foundation gives a yearly prize for the best design in modern furniture.

The Permanent Industrial Exhibition is the place to see what Denmark is doing today with the arts of peace, and the place to see what it did yesterday is the Museum of Applied Arts (Kunstindustrimuseet).

For the foreigner in Denmark eager to become acquainted with the background of Danish taste, this museum is full of suggestion, particularly if, threading his way through the rich labyrinth of medieval, renaissance, baroque, rococo, and ceramic rooms, he will hold fast to the Danish clue. For the Museum is arranged to show not only the development of Danish art and handicraft from the Middle Ages up to the present day, but its connexion—continuous and contemporary—with similar crafts in Europe. Like a sturdy cord running through the silken skeins of French glass painting, Italian majolica, and Delft faience, the Danish characteristics are traceable; the admirable use of woods that are neither rare nor costly; the eschewing of extremes of style; the incorporation of dignity and balance in the common articles of common use.

What enjoyment of the creature comforts is implied by the mammoth porcelain platters which held the mammoth meals of nobles and rich burghers, and by the carved and canopied beds where they slept so soundly under their feather puffs! These wrought-iron gates with their flat filigree flowers, these huge iron locks and bolts and keys protected householders and household riches from marauders in an age before there was security, social or otherwise, in Denmark or anywhere else. Here are chunky cradles which swung chunky babies, carved chests which the housewives dusted diligently, and great clocks which told them when they should go to work and with equal impartiality told them when they could stop. Here, through these rooms, marches a pageant of substantial and jolly living. Here is the tangible expression of a prosperous and well-educated people.

An earlier angle on these same people is given at Lyngby, a little way out from Copenhagen, in one of those open-air Folk Museums of which the Scandinavians seem to have found the happy secret.

The buildings which compose this reconstructed community are from various parts of Denmark and from various eras. The chimneyless dwelling from Jutland is from the second century; the seaman's cottage from Fanö has Dutch tiles set in its walls; from Amager is a room with a wainscoting of inlaid panels and Chinese porcelain brought home by some seafaring owner. Folk costumes, too, are preserved here, and so are the embroideries of the women and the wood carving of the men done in leisure hours to decorate their beds and tables and mangle boards and chairs, and now respectfully studied by modern artists and craftsmen for their designs and colours.

The household furnishings at the Museum of Applied Arts date from the Middle Ages. The houses at Lyngby and the articles in them are of extreme antiquity. And if, having seen these, one is interested to know what manner of Danes lived in Denmark even longer ago, at the National Museum there is a series of rooms which, with its prehistoric relics, surpasses any other in Northern Europe. The ethnological section of this extraordinary institution will be referred to in the chapter on Greenland. But the section of antiquities is sufficient for one chapter and for one day. As one examines the flint implements from the old Stone Age and the polished axes from the new Stone Age, as one marvels at the belt plates with spiral ornaments from the Bronze Age, the bows and arrows, shields and armour from the period of the migration of the tribes, one realizes that from prehistoric time through the decline under Celtic rule, through the quickening under Roman contact, through the Viking period, there have been artist craftsmen in Denmark.

It is possible that some of these tall figures in coarsely woven woollen garments with fur rugs over them, lying on their backs in coffins hewn out of half a mighty oak, were those who hammered the double disks of bronze mounted with gold of the sun car and fashioned these small boats of gold, beaten to the thinness of paper, perhaps as gifts to the gods. It may be that some of them rode in yonder religious processional cart with its ornaments of mounted bronze, or sailed in that boat twelve metres long, its thin planks stitched together—the earliest vessel known in all Scandinavia, and discovered, surrounded by spears and swords and wooden shields, after the Great War, in the island of Als, in what had been a lake and is now a bog.

In the midst of these bright fragments of gold and silver, bronze and glass, a little removed from the sombre oak sarcophagi, there lies upon a bed of earth the shadowy skeleton of a woman. Since before the birth of Christ she has lain thus, with her long gold hairpins on either side her forehead, her right hand lightly under her cheek and on its finger a gold wedding ring. Near her is a wooden vanity case with a comb and pins of bone, scissors and knife of bronze. A bronze kettle which held a fermented drink—the sediment of berries and fibres of flowers are still there—and a cup of Roman glass are close by lest she should thirst during her long waiting in dateless night. Statelily arrayed in her jewellery, with her intimate trinkets cosily within reach, she lies, not on her back as the warriors in their oaken coffins, but a little on one side with her feet crossed at the ankles in a position so soft, so gentle, so utterly feminine that after two thousand years her almost obliterated form retains an ineffable tenderness. She was not young, the inscription tells us, and she had long been ill. Probably born and certainly buried in Jutland, over this vanished corporeality beats Dante's measure: "Never did nature or art present to thee pleasure such as the fair limbs wherein I was inclosed: and they are scattered in earth. And if the supreme pleasure thus failed thee through my death, what mortal thing ought then to have drawn thee to its desire?"

Whoever laid her thus in her grave, thousands of years ago, whoever lifted her from that grave and placed her thus in this impersonal room far from "the busy hum of men," revealed a certain intuitive recognition which is constantly and purely struck in the best of Danish art—so purely, indeed, that one personifies Denmark always as a feminine and not a masculine figure. Always a motherland and not a fatherland; and a woman and not a girl.

Standing beside this faintly outlined form in the Museum room, we recall one of the most penetratingly tender stories of a woman's nature ever incarnated in any language. It was the same Jacobsen who pityingly and inexorably delineated Marie Grubbe, who tells the brief tale of a widow who, in middle age, finding the true love of her life, begs her two grown children, Tage and Elinor, for their sanction and blessing upon her second marriage. This, in the hardness of their young hearts, they refuse her. In grief, but without faltering, Mrs. Fönss leaves her children and goes with her husband and for five years lives happily with him in Spain. Then suddenly she falls ill.

Dear children [she writes], I know that you will read this letter, for it will not reach you until after my death. Do not be afraid, there are no reproaches in these lines; would that I might make them bear enough love.

When people love, Tage and Elinor, little Elinor, the one who loves most must always humble himself, and therefore I come to you once more, as in my thoughts I shall come to you every hour as long as I am able. One who is about to die, dear children, is very poor; I am very poor, for all this beautiful world, which for so many years has been my abundant and kindly home, is to be taken from me. My chair will stand here empty, the door will close behind me, and never again will I set my foot here. Therefore I look at everything with the prayer in my eye that it shall hold me in kind memory. Therefore I come to you and

beg that you will love me with all the love which once you had
for me; for remember that not to be forgotten is the only part
in the living world which from now on is to be mine; just to be
remembered, nothing more.

I have never doubted your love; I knew very well that it was
your great love, that caused your great anger; had you loved me
less, you would have let me go more easily. And therefore I want
to say to you, that should it happen some day that a man bowed
down with sorrow come to your door to speak with you concerning me, to talk about me to relieve his sorrow, then remember that no one has loved me as he has, and that all the happiness
which can radiate from a human heart has come from him to
me. And soon in the last great hour he will hold my hand in
his when the darkness comes, and his words will be the last I
shall hear. . . .

Farewell, I say it here, but it is not the farewell which will be
the last to you; it I will say as late as I dare, and all my love will be
in it, and all the longings for so many, many years, and the memories of the time when you were small, and a thousand wishes and
a thousand thanks. Farewell Tage, farewell Elinor, farewell until
the last farewell.

Your Mother.

Porcelain statuettes and silver spoons for houses which
women caress into homes! Hand-woven curtains and carved
cradles for a land whose very contour suggests the heart's surrender.

CHAPTER FOUR

BUILDINGS AND BUILDERS

THERE are few contradictions in this small and homogeneous land. As the fine arts reflect the Danish scene and the applied arts express Danish taste and character, so the buildings—the old and the new—are in harmony with the national temper.

Thus it is appropriate that the Town Hall (the Raadhus) should suggest a rich burgher mansion; that the Royal Palace most affectionately regarded by Danes is Fredensborg, which is associated with the domesticity rather than the officialdom of kings and queens; that castles should be converted into club houses and sanatoria for the general use of the people; that the sensational new Grundtvig Church should become the centre of a co-operative housing project; and Christiansborg Palace, the supreme monument to absolute monarchy, should be the administrative centre of a Government so democratic that it no longer creates or even bestows titles.

The visitor to a Danish city immediately notices the unostentatious solidity of the large buildings—old-fashioned residences and modern offices alike. In the country he observes

Ninety per cent of the population of Copenhagen live in flats. The balconies of the newer dwelling blocks are ingeniously arranged to provide privacy.

ALLEGHENY COLLEGE LIBRARY

The Grundtvig Church presents a colossal magnification of the traditional corbie-stepped gable.

ALLEGHENY COLLEGE LIBRARY

Copenhagen, while cherishing ancient buildings, is hospitable to
modern architecture.

ALLEGHENY COLLEGE LIBRARY

Professor Niels Bohr, originator of the modern atomic theory.

ALLEGHENY COLLEGE LIBRARY

the suitability of cottages and villas to the topography of the land and the convenience of the occupants. Everything seems to grow out of the soil and out of the necessities of the general life.

There are not many old buildings—in the European interpretation of that word—in Denmark. Copenhagen, swept by successive fires, claims survivals only from medieval times. The village churches, with their distinctive stepped gables, date from the seventeenth and eighteenth centuries, and some of the outlying castles from the thirteenth.

To look down on Copenhagen from the air is to see successive chapters of history spreading out from it like rings from a dropped pebble. The oldest part—the inner city (which originally was a circle with the Kongens Nytorv as its centre) —is still a tangle of winding streets. Here are the famous architectural mementoes of that great builder, Christian IV: the Bourse, with its twisted dragon-tail spire, the Church of St. Nicolaj, the Round Tower—originally an observatory—the Church of Holmen, Rosenborg Castle, and the Regensen, where the University students used to live.

Beyond this congestion of the Middle Ages, circles the Renaissance town with its wider, straighter streets and quadrangular pattern, its climax in the octagonal Amalienborg, with its four corresponding Palaces occupying four sides of the octagon and four streets piercing the other four sides. Frederik's Hospital, which now houses the Museum of Applied Arts and the Music History Museum, also dates from this period. After the bombardment of 1807 the town was rebuilt in austere classicism and the old Nyboder Quarter, which Christian IV had laid out to house the men of his navy, was remodelled to conform to the more symmetrical planning of the city and to take care of the workers who came flocking from the country to get employment in the factories.

The city continued to expand and after the cholera epidemic in 1853 the Medical Society raised tenements beyond the ramparts suitable for people of modest means. This was the beginning of the present new suburbs with their tall—comparatively speaking—apartment houses and straight traffic arteries. Now lakes and parks replace the curved line of the old ramparts.

Thus Copenhagen, with Danish common sense, has adapted itself to changing conditions and yet maintained its continuity of character.

As in any city which has been lived in for centuries and adjusted to changing requirements, the old buildings are crowded with details absorbingly significant to architects, artists, and historians. But in this day of modernistic ideas, the average visitor may be more interested to see what is being done with new materials and new designs.

And he will begin with the Town Hall which was completed in 1905, after eleven years of building—the fifth Town Hall that Copenhagen has known. It stands in a central plaza —who would believe that not so very long ago this spot was the Western Gate and marked the boundary of the capital?— its tall clock tower the tallest of all the city's tall towers.

Robust and splendid, in harmony with the architecture around it, its main outline is somewhat reminiscent of buildings in central Italian towns. In its great "scallop shell" in front, half Copenhagen can stand: in its galleried main hall—really a glass-covered central court—two thousand can be seated to watch the civic festivals.

Martin Nyrop, the architect, whose bust is in the entrance,

had a definite conception not only of what this building should accommodate, but what it should symbolize. It should accommodate the five Mayors and the five Aldermen and the fifty-five members of the City Corporation, the eight hundred people in the offices, and the eight hundred bicycles in the basement. It should symbolize Denmark's distinctive materials and motives. It should have a place for every modern convenience: lifts, electric lighting, central heating—and maintain ancient dignity.

He has done admirably.

The distinction of the Town Hall rests not upon bizarre innovations or upon imitation of other countries, but upon genuineness: genuineness of material and genuineness of workmanship. This is strengthened by Nyrop's appreciation of the handicrafts—even the keys and keyholes are given elaborate form—and by his determination to handle new problems straightforwardly. He does not conceal lifts and electric lighting and central heating, but treats their function as part of the design.

The Town Hall is Danish. It is Danish in its unbroken kinship with the older buildings of Copenhagen, in its congeniality with European tradition, in its unaffected approach to new conditions and its suitability to large gatherings of the people—for unlike a palace with its gates of exclusion, the Raadhus suggests a rich and hospitable burgher house. It is Danish in its symbolism: the national red and white colours in the central hall, the decorative motives of native flora and fauna, the watchmen and polar bears on the merlons, and the beloved three towers everywhere. And finally it is Danish in the busy, unhurried movement of the life within.

For while the Mayors sign papers and the Committees meet

and the clerks place their bicycles in the racks prepared for them and the old age pensioners receive their stipends with self-respecting matter-of-factness, a woman is domestically polishing the brass balustrades and grilles that give a fairy touch to this splendid substantiality. It takes her a fortnight to go from top to bottom and when she has finished she begins all over again, and so, presumably, do Mayors and clerks, Committees and pensioners, when they reach the end, begin all over again. Thus practicality and handsome comfort, housewifeliness and fairy-book gold, social legislation and national symbols merge in the atmosphere of the Town Hall.

The Danishness is not so easily analysed in the other modern building which all foreigners are expected to see. This is the Central Police Station (Politigaarden), its drab walls monotonously pierced by windows of uniform size, its façade unrelieved except for the gold fire-brands—the mark of the police department—on either side the entrance. It may be that the architects (Hack Kampmann, H. J. Kampmann, A. Rafn, and H. Jacobsen) felt that a building in such an unimpressive location, surrounded by heterogeneous structures, should be noncommittal in its street exterior. At any rate, these grey walls are almost depressingly plain.

One enters through a limestone vestibule, by dark low-stepped stairs, and is suddenly confronted by a vast and topless court, like a great Roman circus, around which march pairs of severe columns and out of which open many offices. This stunning architectural climax is totally unexpected. The circular effect is accentuated by the three sharply projecting uniform modillion cornices, whirling in horizontal lines around the complete perimeter. One leaves this sunny circular court, enters a sombre corridor, leading along the axis of the building, and again a surprise is presented. For here is another court, square and shadowy, with eight gigantic columns carrying a heavily ornamental ceiling with a square unglazed aperture in its centre. It is almost like some strange and grandiose rock temple. A niche in the end wall holds Utzon-Frank's statue of Justice, but with this exception the walls are bare. Offices opening out of the courtyards face the street, each with four white walls and a blank white ceiling.

There is no question that the Police Court is effective. It is pertinent to note, however, that what might appear to the casual visitor as daringly modernistic is in actuality more or less a return to the Empire style of 1800.

The Town Hall is a successful combination of tradition and modern practicality. The Police Station is an interesting combination of functionalism in plan and neo-classicism in style. But many of the new flat houses, co-operative apartments, villas, and schools—especially the new University at Aarhus—are frankly modernistic as that word is generally understood everywhere today. And in certain instances very successfully so.

Between a third and fourth of the entire population of Denmark live in Copenhagen and 90 per cent of the population of Copenhagen live in flats. Obviously such congestion calls for wise building regulations, and city architects are hoping to put teeth in the new law requiring that a quarter of the space in all apartment houses must be left open for the children to play in. (There is such a provision in the existing law, but it is not strictly enforced.)

In a land of dark winters the new law regulating the height of any building to not more than half the distance between it and the opposite building needs no defence and bears further relation to the traffic problem and the general character of the capital. There is a definite effort to spread the city out as far as possible and to place tall buildings only where they will not obstruct the light from others and where there is some rationality in having many stories. The new Vestersöhus, its balconied façade overlooking the lake, is an example of such sensible location. Also the idea of what a park should be has changed in the last five or six years. Such breathing spaces are no longer considered primarily as decorations, but as health centres. In the poorer sections of the city these have playgrounds, wading pools, ball fields, and so forth, as in Nörrebro Park.

In a city of this size there are, naturally, flats for every type of purse, the cheapest ones far superior to tenements in American and English cities, and the expensive ones much less elaborate than their counterparts in New York and London. Thus in Hornbäkhus, which is a co-operative tenement put up immediately after the War at a minimum of expense, two- or three-room apartments are attainable for seven or eight hundred kroner a year. It is designed around a very large court, intended principally for quiet and cleanliness rather than utilitarian purposes, as the children's playgrounds, drying yards, and so forth are inconspicuously fitted in along the edge, leaving the central lawn clear. Going up the scale, there are newer municipally owned blocks containing four hundred odd flats and also built around courts. Here four rooms with central heat, common laundry facilities, storage for bicycles and coal, rent for nine hundred and sixty kroner a year. A step further, and there is the privately owned type of flat house, like Storgaarden, with its balconies so ingeniously arranged that they provide absolute privacy and so designed that they are a strikingly effective architectural feature. In such a type of building two rooms, a kitchenette, and a bath would be about one thousand kroner a year.

There is no housing shortage in Copenhagen. Flats of every grade, owned co-operatively, municipally, or privately, are available, and the same is true in the suburbs where single, double, and block houses are going up, pleasingly proportioned, their modernistic plainness relieved by balconies and window boxes, their red tiled roofs and white walls bringing them into the general picture of the Danish countryside.

Each community has its own building regulations, which are very simple in the rural districts, and in the provincial towns are patterned more or less upon the laws of Copenhagen. And in Copenhagen, incongruously enough, the laws of 1889 are still sacrosanct. Thus in an age of stoves it was forbidden to heat or sleep in a room above the sixth story for fear of fire and this law has not been repealed. Buildings higher than six stories use the upper floors for storage purposes. (One ingenious man utilized such a lofty chamber for a dancing school, as the pupils presumably would not need heat or go to sleep.) While working for newer statutes the architects in the interim—like the Mohammedans who dare not use the train to go to Mecca because that method of locomotion is not specifically approved in the Koran—are obliged to refer to laws formulated before cement was known as a building material, and the city planners to conform to provisions drawn up before the multiplicity of bicycles.

The country, too, has its problems. Since a corrugated tin roof is quicker to put on than thatch and cheaper than tile and carries a lower fire insurance rate, too many farmers are adopting this ugly material, oblivious of the fact that the thin metallic substance looks as out of place atop an old cottage

with half-timbered whitewashed walls as a shiny permanent
wave on a meek Madonna.

Also, some of the restoration of the ancient buildings is
being carried on a bit too diligently for the lover of the mel-
lowed antique, and the old windmills—always the most delightful landmarks in a low-lying terrain—are gradually disappearing. But granting these lapses in taste or judgment,
there are still enough thatched roofs and still enough windmills to infuse the countryside with soft distinction. A sufficient proportion of the new flats and villas conform to the
traditional low lines and red-tiled roofs to be in keeping with
the old, and often continue the fashion of affixing the date of
the erection of a house at one end, its name at the other end,
and its street number in front—a documentation probably
necessary if the Hansens and Jensens are ever to sort themselves out.

"Towns, palaces, and cities fine" have done exceptionally
well in preserving medieval charm and accepting modern advancement. Domestic and rural architecture is so excellent
that the eyesores are conspicuous. And in one instance Denmark has achieved something absolutely unique.

The Grundtvig Church, designed by P. V. J. Klint, started
in 1921 and not yet completed, is both modernistic and traditional; it is Gothic and not Gothic; it is kin to every ancient
village church in Denmark and is like no other church in
the world.

On the highest ground in the outskirts of Copenhagen—
Bispebjerg Hill—there rise what seem to be the pipes of a
gigantic church organ. Although the first glance of this steeple
—for that is what it is—seems violently original, at the second
glance we perceive that it is merely a colossal magnification of

the familiar corbie-stepped gable. The steeple with its vertical recesses is of yellow brick. So are the walls of the church inside and out; so are the floors, the arches, the vaults, the columns. With the exception of the wooden furniture and the steel window frames, every single feature—interior or exterior —in this vast edifice is yellow brick. These bricks are not concealed or covered in any way. The eye follows hundreds and hundreds of courses, sees the columns in repeated succession drawn up in mathematical array. The effect is one of unity and strength, and the variety created by the play of light is tremendous. Holding steadily to this architectural motive, "redoubling and trebling it and turning it into a grand composition with the exactitude of a crystal," Klint has evolved a style that is superb. As Steen Eiler Rasmussen says, "He turned mathematics into art and art into mathematics."

With equally sure hand Klint produced not a true Gothic vault or the imitation of a Gothic vault, but an engineer's construction of a vault. And he has used not one Gothic tower but three, which, while unprecedented, is logical for a building with two aisles and a nave.

This absolutely original, absolutely effective ecclesiastic edifice is given additional height and its verticality is emphasized by the long horizontal lines of many one-story dwelling houses which surround it in regular units. This co-operative housing project was also designed by Klint and repeats the similar detail and similar material.

There is nothing fantastic about this extraordinary church and its related village. Everything is consistent, clear, and integral. Nothing could be added or subtracted or, one feels, imitated. It is authentically noble.

Steen Eiler Rasmussen, who is known to English readers

and architects by his delightful book on London, has wittily summarized the paradox of the building and its builder. In the first place, Klint was an engineer, not turning to architecture until he was forty years old, and he designed the Grundtvig Church after he was sixty. He ignored the Academy and his followers founded one. There was no demand for such a building and nevertheless he built it. There was no place for it, and he located it on a site commanding land and sea. The name of the hill happened to be Bispebjerg and since Grundtvig had been called a bishop, Klint stated that in time it would be taken for granted that the hill had been named for him. Finally, concludes Rasmussen, Klint started with a chapel which became a cathedral and ended with a cathedral which became a town, and the man who was not an architect created the most original architectural monument in Denmark today.

PART V

Islands in the Sea

CHAPTER ONE

GREENLAND, THE FAROES, AND ICELAND

SURROUNDED by frozen seas which are patrolled by icebergs, with a curtain of fog between it and the rest of the
world, lies Greenland, a colony of Denmark, and sixty times
larger than its motherland.

It is three thousand nautical miles from Copenhagen to
Upernivik, the most northerly settlement, and with a fast
vessel it takes twelve days to make the voyage. Since it is usually necessary to stop for water and fuel, and since storms,
gales, fogs, and icebergs may intervene, it is seldom reached
within that length of time. It may be entered only by those
who have obtained special permission from the Danish Government, and this is not granted unless their purpose has been
approved on scientific or artistic grounds. For Greenland is a
closed country and for that as well as certain other reasons is
of peculiar interest.

Denmark has had many colonies in her day. The Orkneys
and Shetland belonged to her and, until she sold them to the
United States in 1917, the Virgin Islands in the West Indies.
Iceland was once under Danish rule and, for that matter, so

was another island—England. Today only the Faroes, which are considered as a province, and Greenland remain to her. And this largest island in the world, upon whose surface could be placed Spain and France and Hungary and Germany—in this country which is still partly in the Ice Age—she has for nearly a hundred years been conducting a unique colonial experiment. This experiment, under which the Greenlanders are quietly progressing in knowledge and prosperity and, it is hoped, in health, will be appreciated when history is written in terms of welfare instead of warfare.

The history of Greenland may be said to start in 877, when Gunbjörn, sailing from Iceland, set his foot upon that barren shore. When Erik the Red, outlawed from Iceland, explored it (983), it was inhabited by Eskimos. Erik returned (986) with thirty-five ships and founded the East Settlement in the Julianehaab District and the West Settlement around Godthaabsfjord. In 1261 the Greenland Republic voluntarily declared its submission to the throne of Norway, but with bad times communication between the two fell away. When, several hundred years later, the Settlements were again discovered, the Icelanders who had managed to exist for five centuries in a country bordering on the North Pole had disappeared and it took more than two centuries to regain the geographical knowledge that had disappeared with them. It was only with the great Northwest Passage expeditions to India that Greenland was re-discovered.

From that time to now there is no dearth of information. Explorers, missionaries, and traders have trodden upon each other's heels and as there seems to be something about Greenland which makes everyone who visits it write a book, the bibliography regarding this remote country is remarkably full. There also seems to be something about Greenland which makes people write at prodigious length: reports swell into volumes, diaries assume the proportions of dictionaries, and expeditions are recorded in encyclopædias. Glaciologists, archæologists, mineralogists, ethnologists, pedagogues, and even botanists have written in English, Dutch, French, Norwegian, Swedish, Danish, Icelandic, German, and even in Greenlandish. Novelists have described it. Rockwell Kent has pictured it. From the first description which appeared in the *King's Mirror* (*Kongespejlet*) in the thirteenth century to Birket-Smith's *Eskimos* published a few months ago, the stream has kept up. And for all this, the average person is more or less uninformed about Denmark's experiment in colonization.

Only narrow strips along the coasts of Greenland are habitable. The interior (84 per cent) is covered by a mighty ice cap one thousand—in some places three thousand—metres thick. The remaining 16 per cent is treeless, with a vegetation so meagre that anyone who is not a botanist wonders what these scientists find to write about with such enthusiasm. Seventeen thousand people are scattered on barren shores as long as from Skagen to Lisbon—one thousand of them on the East Coast. About three thousand are Eskimos and the rest a mixed race of Eskimos and Europeans. Although the southernmost part of Greenland is in the same latitude as the northernmost part of Scotland, the climate is Arctic.

What is there of commercial value to Denmark in such a possession? The cryolite mine—the only one of any size yet discovered on the globe—yields annually thirty thousand tons

of this material which is used in the manufacture of enamel
and opal glass and in the making of aluminum by the electro-
lytic method.

Besides the cryolite there is marble, coarse-grained but with
crystals of brilliant and varied colours and adapted for building and sculpture. There is also some so-called brown coal
(lignite) lying between layers of sandstone and slate and of
this coal five thousand tons are mined yearly. Finally there are
the furs from the polar bear and fox, skins from the seal, pelts
from the sledge dogs—and fish. Most of the cod is salted for
export; shark liver, rich in vitamins, is turned into oil for
Danish cattle; whale blubber and shark skins have a steady
market.

Denmark would not be Denmark if she did not make the
best practical use of these natural resources. But the surprising
fact remains that her chief interest in Greenland seems to be
not commercial but scientific—and scientific with more than
a touch of humanitarianism.

As civilization spreads over the earth, primitive peoples
have a way of disappearing. Native tribes which have maintained themselves and developed their unique culture during
thousands of years have degenerated

> "Before this strange disease of modern life,
> With its sick hurry, its divided aims."

And with the disappearance of these tribes—some of them
brave and ingenuous, some of them splendid in physique and
friendly in spirit—have been lost not only tangible realities
but those intangible ones not less precious because "the
world's coarse thumb and finger failed to plumb."

With the ideal of preserving the Eskimos, Denmark made

Greenland a closed country: not only preserving their bodies
from the diseases which the white man brings but preserving
their tiny ethnic and artistic contribution. Such preservation
did not mean that the Eskimos were to be kept in their original state to serve as curiosities. Its intention has been and
still is to help them to develop along logical economic and
intellectual lines so that they will ultimately be able to meet
the other races of the world upon firmer, fairer ground than
has been accorded primitive peoples before.

Here, as in most far, foreign domains, the missionaries came
early. Hans Egede, who was born in Norway, not only built
himself a house at Godthaab in 1721, but made such a thor-
ough study of the country and the people that his findings are
still, after two hundred years, the basis for all Greenland
investigators. He discovered and described the lost Norse colonies, and the more recent recovering from a thirteenth-cen-
tury grave in West Greenland of a bishop's ring and a bishop's
crook carved from a walrus tooth indicates that long before Hans Egede, other holy men had come to save the souls
of the Greenlanders according to the Christian gospel. Today
the Lutheran Church is the centre of every village and the
majority of the priests, whose duties are manifold and arduous,
are native Greenlanders. They receive their preliminary
training, board and tuition free, at the Seminary in Godthaab
and complete it in Denmark. While a few Danish priests are
sent out from Denmark, the native Greenlanders are given
every encouragement to undertake this profession as they have
the advantage of understanding the language and psychology
of their countrymen. Today brides in sealskin trousers and
bead collar capes go through the same marriage promises
as their sisters in Denmark, only in Greenland these prom-

ises are never broken, for divorce is unknown. On December twenty-fourth the fur-clad children celebrate Christmas around a Christmas tree, and while congregations in Scotland and Canada are singing "From Greenland's icy mountains," those in Julianehaab are singing "Hark! the herald angels." And, just to show they are broad-minded, on occasions the Eskimos lift their voices in Bishop Heber's hymn.

The modern missionary serves, in an emergency, as a doctor, and the doctor serves at all hours and in all seasons as a messenger of light as well as healing. Physicians are paid a fixed salary by the State, but only a crown in Heaven can reward them adequately for trips by motor boat in summer, by dog sledge in winter, to hamlets scattered along the illimitable coast line beaten by gales and obscured by fogs. There are fourteen hospitals free to all patients, each in the charge of a Danish trained nurse who, with the local physician, teaches native nurses and finds them competent and sympathetic. Every year dentists are sent up from Denmark to travel from settlement to settlement not only to treat teeth but to teach the care of them. Preventive instruction is also part of the assistance given in the sanatoria for children and those for tubercular patients. Infectious diseases take dangerous forms among primitive people and when, in 1935, a ship on which there was measles was denied entrance, Denmark felt her policy of strict control over all boats was vindicated.

Churches, hospitals, and then schools.

As in the other two cases, natives who show aptitude in the High School and Seminary at Godthaab are sent to Denmark for two- or three-year continuation courses. Today there is a teacher for every fourteen children: school attendance is obligatory and there are no illiterates. There is not even the ordinary quota of dunces, to judge by the alert, inquisitive little faces.

Supplementing the books are manual training—carpentry for boys, sewing and lace-making for girls—and encouragement in those handicrafts which are peculiar to the country. For generations the Greenlanders have been skilful in carving in soapstone and bone, weaving the long grasses which are used between the inner and outer soles of their boots into baskets and trays, elaborately beading the cape collars which crown the native costume, and working in leather—white, scarlet, and blue. The designs always follow mathematical patterns, some of them very intricate. There is no attempt to reproduce the forms of men or animals. And, of course, there are school bands and school dances.

Spiritual guidance is not enough, medical care is not enough, school education is not enough. The Greenlanders must be helped to help themselves practically, and sheep farming has been introduced into a country where seals are decreasing and where climatic conditions are not suitable for cattle.

In 1915 one hundred and eighty sheep were brought in from Iceland and there are now ten thousand. Central stations have been established to teach young Greenlanders how to raise, breed, and herd, and how to make hay for winter fodder. After three years' training, they are given a certain number of sheep to start their own sheep farms and these they pay back in lambs once they are established. The sheep can graze out for the greater part of the year and it is a rather interesting fact that when the lambs are slaughtered they weigh more than half again as much as Icelandic lambs because the Greenland grass is of such good quality.

All these various activities require administrative control. The country is divided into thirteen districts and these are divided into sixty-four communes and in each of these the adult population chooses a council to which Greenlanders and Danes are elected under the same rules, the former being kept in the majority. Each district also has a chairman and two Danish and two Greenland justices who investigate crimes and confer with the Government as to punishment—not a heavy task, for crime is rare and there are no prisons.

The ships which carry all the imports and exports are owned or chartered by the Danish Government and the shops which supply the people with the commodities they need are Government-owned. Prices are fixed to make the necessities available to all. Luxuries are at a minimum and the sale of alcohol is prohibited.

Although ships are the only means of transportation to the country and although boat in summer and sledge in winter will for a long time to come be the only method within the country, the radio brings daily news from Copenhagen which is transmitted all over Greenland and in every settlement is immediately posted for the general information of all. It may be added that the Greenlanders politely reciprocate the radio message from Copenhagen by sending back their daily news. The wireless station is of special value for meteorological reports and shipping, and if more communication is needed, why, there are two newspapers published in Greenland, written and printed by Greenlanders, to be sure, but—for Denmark watches all—published at public expense and delivered free of charge everywhere.

This, then, is Greenland today. It may not function perfectly in every department. Cynics remark that the cryolite mine, employing only Danes, is run by a private concession and in the last ten or fifteen years has yielded a profit of a million and a half kroner annually. To this the retort courteous is that this money is turned back directly into the development of the country. Also in the course of two hundred years much Danish blood has been infused so that the purity of the Eskimo race is by no means intact. Finally, there is the complaint from Norway that Denmark acted unfairly in regard to the Norwegians in Greenland. This controversy, which extended over many years and filled many pages of print, is by no means insignificant. For its solution proves how war may be avoided and honour maintained by nations which hate war and love honour. It should be checked up in that column—lamentably brief—of credit in the ledger of the League of Nations, and be regarded as a shining example to all the nations of the earth.

Norway claims she discovered Greenland: that Gunbjörn was a Norwegian (sailing from Iceland); that Erik the Red was a Norwegian (outlawed from Iceland); that it was under the Norwegian crown that the Greenland Republic voluntarily placed itself. Hans Egede was a Norwegian and scientific work and exploration up to Fridtjof Nansen was carried on by other Norwegians. During the seventeenth and eighteenth centuries the fishing and hunting expeditions to Greenland were sent out from Bergen. In 1721 Norway and Denmark were united under a common king, and it is from that date that Denmark considered Greenland as Danish. But the Norwegians considered it a Norwegian dependency, since its affairs continued to be conducted in Norway in the offices of the Central Administration. In 1814 Denmark ceded Norway to Sweden (by the Treaty of Kiel) but kept part of Greenland.

How much of Greenland Denmark had a right to claim, whether what had been generally considered as No Man's Land included the coast line where Norwegian interests were predominant, the rights of Norwegian hunters and fishers, the value of Norwegian contributions to the scientific and commercial development of the country—these ran into involved argument. They were only partially solved by the East Greenland Convention of 1924 and the controversy came to a climax when, in July 1931, Norway officially annexed the coast line from 71° 30′ to 75° 40′ and handed police powers over to two Norwegians who had already unofficially claimed this territory and named it Erik Red's Land.

Here was enough of right and wrong, enough of bitterness and political scheming, enough of business interest and historical sentiment to have precipitated a war. And instead of fighting, Norway and Denmark submitted the case to the World Court at The Hague and, what is more, accepted the decision which upheld the Danish claim that the wild life on land and in the sea surrounding Greenland cannot be protected and developed except by regulations covering the whole of the island and surrounding waters, and that the life in the sea on the East Coast of Greenland is of the greatest importance to the population of the West Coast. Surely there could be no better example to Greenland of what civilization ought to mean, and can mean, than this intelligent solution of a difficult problem. And, for that matter, no better example to the world.

Since Greenland is inaccessible, both because of its remoteness and because of Denmark's policy of protection, few foreigners have experienced the fascination which it holds for those who know it. But for anyone who would like an idea more vivid than can be gained from a book or a picture, there is a "Little Greenland" in Copenhagen.

The Ethnographical Museum—which is part of the National Museum—is not only the oldest of its kind in the world (it was started in 1846), but among its multitude of treasures it displays the most complete Eskimo collection yet assembled. Nowhere else is arranged such a panoramic history of the Northern tribes, many of which no longer exist. Here are birch-bark tents and reindeer sledges from Northern Siberia; silver-mounted saddles from Central Siberia; here are kayaks of every tribe from East Greenland to Bering Straits. Here the North American Indian is represented more fully than elsewhere in Europe. In Copenhagen there is an Indian club unique in the world. It is complete with stone head and wooden handle inlaid with genuine wampum beads set lengthwise. And here is "Little Greenland" with its genuine summer tents of sealskin and a genuine winter rock house with its entrance lower than the floor to keep out the cold. In order to show the construction with its cantilever arch, it is without the turf which is usually piled against the outside or the skins which usually cover the inside. The cases contain whale hunting costumes, topographical maps in wood, coats made of bird skins, the feathers softer than fur and the skins chewed by Eskimo teeth until they are free from all oil, and flexible and odourless. It is an accurate and complete exposition of the culture peculiar to a people living on treeless shores, fishing in the open sea, and surrounded by drifting icebergs, seven-eighths of which are invisible under the water and the visible eighth suffused with shades of green and lavender and saffron veined with emerald and riding on a plum-coloured sea.

This same plum-coloured sea surrounds other Danish islands than Greenland.

Three hundred and twenty-five miles west of Norway, one
hundred and seventy-three miles north-west of Scotland, crags
of basalt rise scatteringly and steeply from the North Atlantic.
In prehistoric times the Faroes may have—with Scotland, the
Orkneys, and Iceland—been joined to Greenland. Now they
are not joined even to each other.

A score of islets, their bare promontories falling abruptly
to the water, some of their peaks rearing almost three thousand feet into the sky, chilled by a climate similar to that of the
north of Scotland, with heather, grass, and lichen the most important vegetation and the hare the only wild animal—who
can live in the Faroes?

Twenty-five thousand Faroese not only cling to these jagged
rocks, but even cling to their nationalism and wish to be
considered not Norwegians, from whom they originally descended, not Danish, although they accept the status of a
Danish province, but a separate Northern people as distinctive as those who live in Iceland, Sweden, Norway, Finland,
and Denmark. They are even reviving their native tongue—
more than reviving it, since, in former centuries, it had been
a spoken language only, and not until the nationalistic movement began (1880) was it considered in the schools, the press,
and the churches. Quite recently it has been formulated into
a Faroese-Danish dictionary.

The largest island, Strömö, is thirty miles long and at its
widest part seven and a half miles. In Svinö, one of the smallest, there is one village with two hundred and twenty-six in-

habitants. On Kunö, whose chain of mountains is broken in only one place, the village of Skarö is deserted, for every man who lived in it was lost at sea in 1913. The coast line of Stora Dimon is nowhere less than three hundred feet high and the only ascent is by steps hewn out of the rock, and near by a hoist for bringing sheep and cattle and provisions to and fro. Surprisingly, there is a plateau on the top where a farmer and his family, the only inhabitants of the island, live surrounded by thirty cows and hundreds of grazing sheep. In the winter they are completely cut off from the world and even in the summer communication is possible only in good weather.

Up to 1856 the Faroes were a closed country, as Greenland is today, and the Faroese are an agricultural people under the Royal Danish Trade Monopoly.

Today they gather their harvest from the sea. The windrows which are laid out upon the rocks to cure are windrows not of grass but of cod, and the gathered crop is not hay but the famous klip-fish, or dried cod, shipped to Denmark and Spain and other fish-loving countries. In fact, although the population of the Faroes is less than 1 per cent of the total population of Denmark, the fish caught by the men of the Faroes totals 40 per cent that of the entire kingdom. There are two fishing seasons—from February to May south of Iceland, from June to October east of Iceland—and these two seasons are two prolonged life-and-death campaigns in which men fight day and night against the elements. The traditional ship is a kind of smack carrying twelve or fourteen men, but gradually schooners are being adopted. These carry as large a crew as thirty and usually have auxiliary engines. But even with this advance the labour is hazardous, prodigious, and poorly recompensed. Two thousand kroner a year is as much as the best fisherman may hope for, while the average is lucky if he earns twelve hundred.

Cod furnishes the living of the Faroese, but the whale furnishes the sport: not the larger mammals which are dealt with by whalers with cannon firing the explosive harpoons, but the smaller ca'ing whale which during the summer comes in herds to these waters. When such a herd is sighted the whole community rushes out: men run to the shore, launch their boats, prepare their gear, and, with the precision brought by generations of experience, drive their quarry toward the land and up into a fjord where escape is blocked. If possible, they force it up on the shore. If this is not possible, it is killed in the water amid shouts and spear thrusts and blood and flying harpoons and capsized boats as wild as any Viking bout. After the slaughter, meat and blubber are divided impartially among all the families of the community whether or not their men were in the hunt.

Besides fishing and whaling, the Faroese raise sheep, and these they do not shear but pluck, waiting until the time of year when the wool is about to be shed and then simply pulling it out by handfuls. The women knit it into garments so warm and so attractive in their closely patterned dark blue and black that the few coats and caps that get to Copenhagen are snatched up by connoisseurs.

Bird catching, too, is one of the vocations and avocations, for on the precipitous bluffs nest auk and gull by the myriad. Some of these are shot from boats or netted from boats as they are driven by beaters on the cliff down to the sea. But your true fowler either climbs up the rocks or is let down by a rope from the top and, with a long two-handled net, he scoops

in the startled birds as they whirl past him, or cleverly cap-
tures them by dropping his net about them as they sit sunning
on the ledges. A skilful fowler can net as many as a thousand
birds in a day and if he risks his life with every movement of
his body and with every dislodged stone that comes clattering
down—well, so does he risk it when he spears the ca'ing whale,
and when he sets forth in a little smack to fish the cod from
the icy waters. Eider duck and sea swallows are not caught by
nets but are shot. Their flesh is eaten and their feathers sold
to fill those five-foot quilts which so inadequately cover the
visitor to Denmark.

After they return from fishing for cod, from plucking sheep
and slaughtering whales and netting birds, the Faroese find
time and energy to dance. Here still exist the medieval chain
dances in all their rhythm and measures, accompanied by ballads and epic songs—not a national dance in the sense of having originated here, but a direct descendant, and the only one
left in Europe, from the thirteenth, fourteenth, and fifteenth
centuries. Clasping hands, loosing them to admit newcomers,
clasping them again, the whirling circle expands, contracts,
and assumes strange shapes as it winds among other circling
groups. In accompaniment to the hoarse bass of the narrator
who sings

> *"The Keisar sat on his high-seat*
> *In garments all of gold,*
> *And of all his chosen champions*
> *The foremost was Roland bold,"*

the young and old trip lightly or stamp; pause or trample like
war horses, taking up the refrain:

"Forth from Frankland did they ride,
With jewelled saddles all;
Loud did Roland wind his horn
In Runtsival."

Thus the men and women of the Faroes live, sharing communally in their catch, risking their lives for a bagful of feathers, turning their klip-fish in the sun, and hurrying to bring it in from the rocks before a storm. They are desperately poor. But they are not too poor to have their songs and ballads and to recite them in their own tongue. They are separated from the rest of mankind by fogs and gales, they are lifted out of the North Atlantic on cliffs of basalt. Between them and the lowering skies are roofs of turf, starred with wild flowers, and under these roofs they dance the chain dances of medieval times and sing of Roland and his horn.

Who first inhabited these wild rocks is uncertain. There is a record of recluses from Ireland in the eighth century, the Norwegians arrived in the ninth, and in the tenth the islands came under Norwegian rule. In 1380, together with Norway and Denmark, they were ruled by one King and in 1709 they were annexed to the Diocese of Zealand. When Norway united with Sweden (1814), the Faroes, like Greenland and Iceland, remained under the Danish King. In 1816 a Danish Governor was appointed over them and since 1849 they have been represented in the Danish Government by one member in the Upper House and one in the Lower.

Greenland is a colony of Denmark. The Faroes are a province. But Iceland is a Sovereign State whose King is the King of Denmark. Like Greenland and the Faroes, it was originally colonized by Norwegians and after the separation of 1814 remained under the Danish crown. The present relations between the two countries were defined by the Union Act of 1918, one of the provisions being that Denmark is to safeguard the foreign affairs of Iceland. Danish citizens in Iceland enjoy equal rights and privileges with the citizens of Iceland and vice versa and the citizens of each country are exempt from military service in the other. Access to fishing within the maritime jurisdiction of both countries is equally free to Danish and Icelandic citizens and Danish ships in Icelandic harbours have the same right as Icelandic ships and vice versa.

The very name of Iceland has always intrigued travellers and scholars, rather paradoxically, since hot geysers are more characteristic of it than ice. Although it is no longer a part of Denmark and has no logical place in this book, its association has been sufficient to recall the words of Viscount Bryce in his preface to Stefansson's book on *Denmark and Sweden, with Iceland and Finland:*

Now Iceland is of quite exceptional and peculiar interest, not only in its physical but also in its historical aspects. The Icelanders are the smallest in number of the civilized nations of the world. Down till our own days the island has never had a population exceeding seventy thousand, yet it is a Nation, with a language, a national character, a body of traditions that are all its own. Of all the civilized countries it is the most wild and barren, nine-tenths of it a desert of snow mountains, glaciers, and vast fields of rugged lava, poured forth from its volcanoes. Yet the people of this remote isle, placed in an inhospitable Arctic wilderness, cut off from the nearest parts of Europe by a stormy sea, is, and has been from the beginning of its national life more than 1000 years ago, an intellectually cultivated people which has produced a literature both in prose and poetry that stands among the primitive literatures next after that of ancient Greece if one regards both its quantity and its quality. Nowhere else, except in Greece, was so much produced that attained, in times of primitive simplicity, so high a level of excellence both in imaginative power and in brilliance of expression.

Not less remarkable is the early political history of the island. During nearly four centuries it was the only independent republic in the world, and a republic absolutely unique in what one may call its constitution, for the government was nothing but a system of law courts, administering a most elaborate system of laws, the enforcement of which was for the most part left to those who were parties of the lawsuits.

In our own time Iceland has for the student of political institutions a new interest. After many years of a bloodless constitutional struggle between its people and the Danish Crown, Denmark conceded to Iceland a local legislature, and an autonomy under that legislature which has greatly improved the relations between those two countries and furnished another argument for those who hold that peace and progress are best secured by the application of the principles of liberty and self-government.

Denmark's colonization in Greenland, Iceland's self-government, the nationalistic movement in the Faroes—these are worth the attention of all who are interested in the new social era. Histories, records of explorations, and tables of figures and facts are roads by which the mind is aided in its approach to an unknown country.

But whoever would approach the soul of a people must see the external world which has produced them not only as scientists describe it but as artists delineate it. The connexion between Nature and man must be interpreted to them not only by economists but by poets. The fearful struggle, the sublime compensations and desolations—in *An Iceland Fisherman* Pierre Loti distilled for all time the strange and radiant and awful beauty of those isolated lands and lives.

Yann goes to sea, as all able-bodied young men in those Northern regions must go to sea, and leaves behind him, as they all must do, a young wife. The story of his voyages and of her waiting is one which is repeated, season after season, year after year, in every little village whose existence depends upon the fishing-boats and whose name is only known in the world by the value of its "catch," and the record of its mortality. "The village of Skarö," says the guide-book, "is deserted, for every man from there was lost at sea in 1913." Some husbands return like wandering birds driven home by the frost, but Yann does not return.

One August night, out off gloomy Iceland, mingled with the furious clamour of the sea, his wedding with the sea was performed. It had been his nurse; it had rocked him in his babyhood, and had afterward made him big and strong; then, in his superb manhood, it had taken him back again for itself alone. Profoundest mystery had surrounded this unhallowed union. While it went on, dark curtains hung pall-like over it as if to conceal the ceremony, and the ghoul howled in an awful deafening voice to stifle his cries. He, thinking of Gaud, his sole, darling wife, had battled with giant strength against this deathly rival, until he at last surrendered, with a deep death-cry like the roar of a dying bull, through a mouth already filled with water; and his arms were stretched apart and stiffened for ever.

All those he had invited in days of old were present at his wedding. All except Sylvestre, who had gone to sleep in the enchanted gardens far, far away, at the other side of the earth.

CHAPTER TWO

BORNHOLM

THESE far half-frozen tracts are not Denmark's only islands. She is surrounded by islands. Professor Achton Friis has visited and, in a three-volume work, described five hundred and twenty-seven, and the tale is not yet told. Yachtsmen and hunters discover new ones every season.

There is, however, one which is different from all the others: different in its geological structure, in its geographical relation to Denmark, in its history and feeling. This is Bornholm.

If Fünen is the middle daughter between Zealand and Jutland, Bornholm is the sturdy small brother in whom, for all his diminutive stature, are firmly developed the doughtiness and undemonstrativeness of a man.

An over-night boat from Copenhagen arrives in the early morning at Rönne, substantially built on rock and out of rock, and yielding not one jot to Copenhagen in its air of self-containment and composure. The whole island of Bornholm is not more than three hundred square miles and in Rönne there are only about eleven thousand people. But it has a large paved market-place and small stout houses: even the Governor's mansion and those of the sea captains and rich merchants

The Bornholm herring are hung in the sun, suspended from low
racks like the tubes of a miniature xylophone.

ALLEGHENY COLLEGE LIBRARY

Whitewashed windmills high-set on a flat terrain give accent to the landscape.

ALLEGHENY COLLEGE LIBRARY

An ancient stump mill on the island of Bornholm.

ALLEGHENY COLLEGE LIBRARY

On a Danish farm. Denmark has the most efficient small farmers in the world. Ninety-two per cent of the agricultural holdings are cultivated by their owners.

ALLEGHENY COLLEGE LIBRARY

are a story or a story and a half, with perhaps a big dormer, and they are tile-roofed and lime-washed like their humbler neighbours. There are two churches with granite doorways as impregnable as fortress gates and an Old People's Home of such handsome proportions and on such an authoritative site that it suggests that even the aged in Bornholm submit to no flimsy substitutes. Rönne also has its Public Library with twenty-two thousand books, and if anyone wants another it is sent from Copenhagen, or from England or Germany for that matter, and received with no delay, for Bornholmers insist that their demands be given prompt attention.

There is something about the situation of this island—lying between Sweden and Denmark—that makes it seem independent of either, something about the fresh Baltic breeze that makes the people brisk and thrifty, something about the rocky structure of their small domain which makes them resolute. For unlike the rest of Denmark, which is as free from rocks as whipped cream is from lumps, Bornholm is all rock. The western shore is as craggy as Cornwall and the seven-hundred-year-old ruined Hammer Castle high on the Hammer headland reminds one of King Arthur's Castle in Tintagel.

Granite is the stern crop, and many a grassy hill has been slashed open into quarries. The granite is cut into blocks or ground into gravel and besides making all the roads of the island as indestructible as iron, it is shipped to Denmark. If one sees a granite paving stone in North Jutland or South Fünen, one can be sure it was quarried in Bornholm and shipped across the Baltic. The local clays are utilized in the pottery factories and their different colours—mahogany, white, and almost black—lend themselves well to those delightful

figures which embody the sentiment and the elemental humour of the island.

For all its crags and cliffs and chasms, for all its granite and
oak, Bornholm is not forbidding. The evenly distributed
meadows and gardens are smooth and fertile, for every man
owns his own farm, and none is so small that it cannot support
its family and none is so large that it cannot be properly cultivated. It is not bleak, for there are many trees, some rarely
found elsewhere in Denmark, and the beautifully kept State
Forest of Almindingen, where in the eleventh century the
Danish rulers had their hunting castles, is the third largest in
the kingdom. Furthermore, Bornholm is sheeted with colour.
Blue chicory and white tansy and red thistles and yellow
golden-rod dance through the pageant of the seasons along
the roadside, and the same clear flower tones are reflected on
the walls of the cottages—the delphinium blue, the rose, and
primrose yellow well set off by the ancient black half-timbers.
On the uplands the purple wild campanula is a forerunner
of the purple heather. Rough granite rocks and smooth granite paving stones are not always under foot. In the south at
Dove Point (Dueodde) between the lighthouse and the sea
lie drifts of sand, dazzling on a sunshiny day and on a cloudy
one shading into tints of green and grey and gold, while
under a paler sky the sea is blond. The dunes heap up and
shift according to the habit of dunes: their bastions crumble
and the familiar beach plants, the stunted pine and birch,
gorse, and creeping grasses cover them.

Before the War many Germans came to Bornholm for their
holidays. Now the summer visitors, whose bright jerseys glint
on the beaches, come chiefly from Denmark proper or from
Sweden. They investigate the Paradise Hills with their ridge

of glacier-scratched granite and hunt for mounds and graves and ancient rune stones and more ancient monoliths in the semi-shadows of Louisenland or in the open fields between Svaneke and Nexö. They climb the granite tower in the Almindingen woods and look out over the whole island, over the planted evergreens, the meadows beyond, and the four round churches from the thirteenth century which are the prized distinction of Bornholm. They find the path to the ruins of Hammerhus where Leonora Christine was so long a prisoner, and look across to Sweden, recalling that for four hundred years it was not the King of Denmark but the Archbishop of Lund or the Hanseatic town of Lübeck that was master of this island. They penetrate the grottoes and caves gouged out from the base of the cliffs and cling to the footpaths on the sides of the crags which drop and leap and arch into the sea. The crags are wild and cracked and seamed but, with their lavender spurs duplicated in lavender shadows in the water below, they are not savage. Surely no woman has wailed here for her demon lover—at least not on a summer day. Perhaps in a storm on a dark night she might wail a little.

Bicyclists wheel along the roads, although these ups and downs are not like the level or the rolling stretches of Zealand and Fünen, and after a few hours of pedalling more than their eyelids must be a little weary. Visitors may motor or cycle or take the train, but a lumbering carriage packed with father and mother and children and drawn by two pounding farm horses shows that the conservative native still finds this method of locomotion entirely satisfactory.

Indeed, the best way to see the island—or at least those fishing villages along the coast which slope crookedly down to the sea—is behind a horse or, better yet, on foot. For the streets in such a village are as independent as the people. They march off in any direction they jolly well please and stop short when they feel like it. And the houses sit themselves down at any angle they jolly well please and elbow their way out on to the sidewalk and the automobilist can accommodate himself to these eccentricities or turn around and go back to Rönne.

It would be a pity to turn back before reaching Tejn where the tang of the spray and drying sails and ropes mingles with another—that of smoked herring.

Herring, herring, who has a herring? Everyone in Tejn has a herring. Everyone in Bornholm has a herring the like of which was never eaten elsewhere. From May until the middle of September they are brought in by the boatload, salted for a few hours and then hung in the sun—glittering rows and rows of them suspended from low racks like the tubes of a miniature xylophone. Then they are carried into queer low sheds with queer round chimneys—the sheds very small, the chimneys very large, like gnome houses. In these dim fumatoria old women in wooden shoes and folded head-dresses— jolly Fates whose duty is not to chop off the thread of human lives but to prolong the flavour of piscatorial—sit before primitive fireplaces sprinkling water on the wood embers. Clouds of smoke billow from the fragrant alder and elder logs, for there is a science to all this as scrupulous as the curing of a Virginia ham. They turn and toast the grills of herring and the smell of the damp wood mingles with the smell of roasting fish and is gradually added to the accumulated aroma of the ceiling, the walls, the floor, and the old women.

Thus are prepared the "röget sild" one sees on all the menu cards and in all the fish store windows in Copenhagen and all over Denmark. Of course, the Bornholmer turns up his nose

at "röget sild" anywhere but in Bornholm. He is convinced
that this specialty of the island loses its prime excellence with
transportation, that it should be eaten within a day or two
after roasting, that it is best smoking hot from the shed. He
regards a "röget sild" as a perishable tropical fruit which
must be plucked at the precise moment of perfection and con-
sumed within an hour. And whoever has eaten a fresh smoked
herring still warm from a Bornholm shed is inclined to agree
with him.

And having reached Tejn one must, of course, go on to
Svaneke, with its granite-walled harbour crowded with white
and green fishing-boats. In front of the little inn is a mulberry
tree, said to be a thousand years old, its gnarled limbs bound
with bands and braced by props, serving as a tea room. Walnut
trees are here, too, figs, snowball bushes, Virginia creeper, and
wild grape-vine. In the courtyard in the rear horses are being
unharnessed from the carryall and beside the wooden pump
and well a cat sleeps in the sun, agreeably full of fish and cream
and kittens.

Whoever does not feel himself far enough away from the
great world in Svaneke can take a packet boat from there and
go farther and fare smaller. The Ertholm Islands are a fistful
of scattered rocks, but the early settlers erected such strong
fortresses on them that they still cast their shadows over the
fishermen and their families who have lived there for two
hundred and fifty years and who have transported enough soil
to have gardens and even trees. There is a bird sanctuary on
Ertholm, just to make sure that the eider duck will not disappear and with it some potential feather quilts.

Whoever has read *Pelle the Conqueror* will go to the village
of Nexö from which the author took his name. Here the gran-

ite disappears and everything is sandstone: the paving blocks of the street, the dry dock in the harbour, the tablets in the graveyard. The cottage where Nexö spent his childhood is pale yellow on a pink base with brown trimmings. There is a garden in back, a field on one side, the sea a little way off, and the road in front. In this cosy little teapot generated the tempest that tore across a thousand pages. From this restricted site Nexö—and Pelle—looked out and saw the horizon of a greater world.

It is a long time since Bornholm belonged to Sweden, but the housewives still address their mops and brooms and scrub-brushes and dust-cloths with an accent and emphasis that is very Swedish indeed. It is longer still since the island was part of what is now Germany, but until a few years ago there might be seen in Arnage, on the jetty walls, specimens of petrified tree stumps from a submarine wood which once connected the then dry land to the continent of Europe.

Now Bornholm prides itself on belonging to itself. It has adopted what it wishes from the rest of Scandinavia. It has co-operative dairies and municipally run hospitals and a Rotary Club and a Folk High School. It calmly declares its cattle are superior to those on the mainland of Denmark, for isolation has made it possible to keep such standards that it is harder for a cow with a cold in her head to get to market than for a camel to pass through the eye of a needle.

The Bornholmers love to leave home and love to return to it. Until twenty-five years ago, when the present excellent boat service between Rönne and Copenhagen was started, a journey to the mainland was a journey indeed. So much so that they still tell the story of the man who, arriving at the capital for the first time, was so impressed that he cabled his wife to

sell the farm, engage passage, and come and join him in that
distant metropolis. Now they travel farther—even to America
—and stay long enough to accumulate a tidy capital and then
go home to take up the old farm and repair the old slate roofs.
They return to the windmills and the lighthouses and the
round churches and to the little harbours that indent the
fishing villages and to the woods of Almindingen. They carry
on their fathers' professions and trades and perpetuate their
fathers' names. They return to the traditions and ancestral al-
legiances which lift the individual life beyond the individual
span.

The granite roads and stone houses withstand the buffetings
of storm and centuries. The pride and thrift of the natives
withstand contact with the transient visitor. Bornholm and
the Bornholmers are founded upon a rock.

PART VI

Denmark in the World

DENMARK IN THE WORLD

THE port of Copenhagen lies in a position of peerless authority at the gateway to the Baltic.

When Bishop Absalon named it Havn—later it was called Köpmannehavn—the Merchants' Harbour—and on the site of the present Christiansborg Castle built his fort to protect it against pirates, he foresaw that this would be the natural port of call for sea-borne trade to and from the Baltic. But Bishop Absalon never previsioned the twenty thousand steam-ships, motor ships, and luxury liners, besides the fishing-boats, lumber barges, freighters, and tankers which yearly make use of the twenty-two miles of docks and quays which line the present water front. He never previsioned the drawbridges, the electric cranes, and all the modern mechanical equipment of what is now the most important harbour of the North. He had never imagined Estonia, Latvia, and Lithuania as in-dependent nations, or heard of America or the Kiel Canal. As for a Free Port—existing as a separate entity within the confines of the Great Port—such an idea was not yet ready for formulation in the brain of even that astute statesman and patriot.

It took a long time for this idea to form in anyone's brain. Until less than a hundred years ago Denmark followed the fashion of the times and collected revenue by merely taking it from passing vessels. As every vessel which entered or left the

Baltic had to sail directly in front of Kronborg Castle, it was easy enough to levy and enforce an arbitrary tribute. It was not until 1857 that a general concert of the nations of Europe forced Denmark to accept a capitulation grant of eighteen million pounds and relinquish what she had come to consider her rightful privilege.

Thereupon Denmark conceived a wiser way not only to enjoy the benefits of Baltic trade, but to attract maritime commerce of far wider dimensions. This was the establishment of a Free Port into which all vessels from all nations could enter without the usual dues and fees which weighed so heavily on shipping elsewhere, but with only a nominal pierage charge. Once inside the Port they could discharge, store, and tranship their goods for any country (except Denmark) without any duty and without Customs authorities examining, delaying, and adding extra charges to the cost of transmission. In 1892 the Royal Charter granted an eighty-year concession to the Copenhagen Free Port Company, Limited, and in 1894 the present Free Port was opened to traffic. The Free Port and the Great Port are, obviously, of mutual advantage to one another.

They share the same geographical position which makes Copenhagen not only the natural port of call and transhipping point for Baltic trade, but another, not so often realized: the sailing distances between Copenhagen and any port north of Panama on the east coast of America are shorter than those between Hamburg and these ports, as a glance at the globe or Philips's Nautical Maps will show, and of course Copenhagen is nearer the Baltic ports than the North Sea coast of Germany. Accessibility to deep water and total absence of tide, making navigation possible at all hours, are shared by both ports.

Besides its unique location, the Great Port of Copenhagen takes its rightful place with all the other great ports of the world in up-to-date equipment. With its bunker coal and bunker oil depots, its stationary, floating, and travelling cranes, its elevators, basins, ship-yards for designing, building, repairing, and cleaning vessels of all types; with its salvage steamers, pilot boats, and tow boats, its railway lines (belonging to the State Railways), its ice breakers, patrol boats, salvage and stevedoring firms, dredges and dumping barges, it has every modern harbour facility and accommodation.

The Free Port occupies the best-equipped and also the deepest section of the entire harbour and may be considered not only as international territory but as a unique township all its own. In addition to harbour equipment so excellent that it makes this the cheapest and quickest port of call in North Europe, it possesses its own post-office, telegraph office, station, branch bank, restaurants, provision dealers, electrical works—even its own railway system which connects with the State Railways and with the ferries to and from Sweden. Since it is not confined to the handling of goods which are to be re-shipped to other countries, its boundaries are guarded by Customs officials, and the handsome building just outside the main entrance is the Custom-House. Its vast warehouses (exceeding two million square feet) include cold storage houses, heated warehouses, and special sheds for the fruit trade. Numbers of merchants and manufacturers have rented sites on the Free Port territory and built offices, warehouses, and factories, taking advantage of manufacturing, storing, and exporting goods unhampered by Customs regulations, "the only stipulation being that manufacturing cannot be carried out within the Free Port without the sanction of the Minister for Public Works."

Just as the Free Port benefits from its own peculiar advantages and from many of those of the Great Port, so it has the advantage of being an international domain and—through effective Government control—enjoying the same security as an official institution. Its administration is not subject to any control of the Government authorities except in regard to warehouse rents and labour charges. These, which are the lowest in Northern Europe, cannot be raised except by special permission of the Danish Government.

Filled with roseate notions about a Free Port, the foreigner is astonished to find that in Denmark itself not only certain imported articles are taxed excessively, but that certain others are practically prohibited—among them American motor cars! And he will not be many days in Copenhagen without hearing the word "Valutacentral." Although he probably will not endeavour to master all the pros and cons of restriction of the import trade in force at present, it is possible he may be inconvenienced by it. If he seeks for an explanation, it will be given him highly coloured by the approval or irritated disapproval of his informant.

If he really wishes to understand why the present Import Licence Scheme, the "Valutacentral"—Nationalbankens Valutakontor—came into existence, he will have to go back to the outbreak of the Great War when the obligation of the Danish National Bank to convert its notes into gold, on demand, was suspended. Here, as elsewhere, the paper standard resulted in a period of inflation followed by a deflationary crisis in the years after 1920. In 1927 Denmark returned to the gold stand-

ard. During the following years the Danish krone was probably overvalued in much the same way as the English pound.
And when Great Britain went off gold, Denmark had to follow suit. England being by far Denmark's principal customer
and the main source of Denmark's export income, the Danish
krone followed the pound sterling in 1931 and after a further
depreciation in 1933 it has been kept at a low but firm rate of
exchange against sterling (about 23 per cent under the rate
of exchange for sterling as against gold). This augmented income has helped to balance the agricultural industry.

In spite of this, Denmark found that she was suffering from
a negative balance of trade. The expenses of imports from
abroad have been larger than income from exports, shipping,
and so forth. In order to meet this problem, the Government
devised the Nationalbankens Valutakontor, whose important
—and difficult—task since February 1932 has been to regulate
and cut down the imports, so that the influx of foreign ex-
changes could be made to cover the expenses for import, interest on foreign loans, and so forth. Obviously, countries
which buy nothing from Denmark are the first to be elimi-
nated as sellers to Denmark. This is the reason that a country
which was previously crowded with American motor cars,
cigarettes, fresh and canned fruit, and gadgets, now buys the
greater part of these things from other countries which offer
greater reciprocity. (In 1934 Denmark bought 82,000,000
kroner's worth of goods from the United States and the United
States 11,000,000 from Denmark. In 1935 the amounts were
69,000,000 as against 9,000,000 respectively.) Inevitably such
a restrictive brake upon free import trade is an annoyance not
only to foreign countries who formerly exported to Denmark,
but to many Danish importers. They find scant consolation in

the fact that the restriction of imports has been advantageous to the home industries of Denmark. Even when they admit these advantages they consider them temporary.

As a matter of fact, the Danish home industries have done extremely well in filling in the empty places. With the exception of a few objects of luxury, there is practically no lack of anything in Denmark, and many things which were formerly imported are now being manufactured similar in appearance, quality, and price. From ship-building to silk stockings and pencils, industry is benefiting from the "Valutacentral": unemployment is relatively small (about 80,000) and the country is prosperous and content. Denmark is meeting her obligations abroad, paying for her imports, paying all amounts due on her foreign loans, and her standing as a debtor nation is very high as may be seen by the rates for Danish bonds quoted in international markets.

The Bourse, which is the oldest in use in Europe, has reared its twisted dragon tails against the sky of Copenhagen since 1610. In these handsome rooms, which extend the width of the building, merchants of fine foreign goods used to gather in their top hats and morning coats, and the booths displaying goods were arranged in the splendid Exchange Hall. Now the Bourse is the place for dealing with stocks and bonds and for supervising the Stock Exchange—which is called the Free Market, with a merchant elected annually as president. No selling in advance is permitted, and the quotation of butter prices is fixed every Thursday by a special committee and this all-important news is telegraphed all over Northern Europe.

But although skilful handling of economics and finance is recognized today as part of any national protection, there still remain the more primitive and visible agencies of defence.

What does Denmark—a country of 3,600,000—do as regards an army and a navy? And precisely what value could these be if any of her mighty neighbours should extend thirsty jaws to lap up that little bowl of cream?

Denmark has an army, schools for commissioned and non-commissioned officers, and an arsenal for the manufacture of munitions. National conscription was introduced in 1849. At the age of seventeen, young recruits are entered upon the conscription rolls and between the ages of nineteen and twenty-five receive their first military training.

According to the present Army Act, which dates from 1932, the period of service in the principal branches of the army is five months, apart from a few training periods of shorter duration later on. . . . The men of the last eight years' service form the Troops of the Line, while those of the previous eight years form the Reserve. During these 16 years the conscripts must keep the enlistment authorities informed as to their address and may not leave the country without permission. Under war conditions the army can be brought up to a total strength of about 100,000; it comprises about 500 permanent officers and 500 to 600 non-commissioned officers, besides a number of reserve officers. . . .

The navy consists of the fleet and the coast-defence organization.

The fleet, which is built more especially for coast defence, comprises a few small battleships, as well as gunboats, torpedo boats, submarines, and minelayers, seaplanes and aeroplanes.

The coast-defence organization comprises a number of sea and land forts, whereas the former fortifications round Copenhagen on the land side have been dismantled.

The total personnel of the fleet and the coast-defence organization in peace time is about 2000, including 270 officers and a number of petty officers, with a training period for the conscripts of six months.

Under war conditions the total personnel of the navy can be brought up to about 8000, including all ranks.

No one—not even the most sanguine Dane—could think that such a small military and such an antiquated naval force, although it might delay, could actually withstand a determined attack by any of the great nations, and there are Danes who argue for complete disarmament. Let Denmark be declared a neutral, they ask, and let England guarantee a safeguard to that neutrality. To answer these in reverse order: First—the question of England's guarantee of Danish neutrality, while mentioned in Danish newspapers when the Locarno Treaty was being negotiated in 1925, has never been discussed *officially*. Second—the right to be considered a neutral by belligerent nations can be maintained only by that neutral doing its utmost to resist aggression and to defend its neutrality.

In late years (and particularly since the Italian-Abyssinian War) Denmark—with Sweden and Norway—has feared that the League of Nations will be an instrument of service only to the great nations. These three Scandinavian countries have declared that they want to formulate their own policy and guard their own interests. They wish to be absolutely out of European entanglements. Their policy is no longer solidarity but neutrality. But—to repeat—the condition upon which any country may be granted the rank of a neutral is by defending itself by force to the utmost of its ability. Therefore, it is necessary for Denmark, like the rest of the world, to maintain an army and a navy. This is the reason for her soldiers, marines, and munitions plants, and for 13 per cent of all national expenditure being used for defence. And this is the reason that twelve thousand nurses (trained by the State) are at present taking special courses for the care of victims of chemical warfare.

"What is the function and value of small nations in the civilization of the world?" asked Edmund Gosse a quarter of a century ago, having in his mind and in his heart Denmark, whom he not only loved—as all who visit her must love her—but whom he understood as few foreigners have ever done.

Perhaps part of the answer will be suggested if we pause before one of those time-softened maps which adorn the many book-shop windows of Copenhagen. Such an ancient chart has a value beyond that of being converted into a pretty lamp shade by a tourist. It may be inaccurate in detail, but it is truthful in showing how Denmark was once the most extensive monarchy in Europe, reaching from the Polar Seas to the Eider, with colonies in the Atlantic and the Caribbean. Those modern maps which hang in shipping offices and on the walls of factories are entirely accurate and equally significant. They show Danish trade routes to ports all over the globe and Danish trade centres in every continent and country. Not in size but in quality Denmark still holds her place among the nations. "What outwardly has been lost shall inwardly be regained."

Within her borders, as well as beyond them, she has applied the same principle of excelling through intelligence and through superiority of production, industrial as well as agricultural. She has succeeded so notably that she is a social laboratory visited in steadily increasing numbers by individuals and delegations seeking to find the best way for man to maintain himself, to care for those who cannot care for themselves, and for all to enjoy the blessings and beauties of this goodly frame, the earth.

What is the value of such a small nation in the civilization of the world? The answer is completed by whoever, loving his own country, also seeks to understand another.

A SHIP SAILS AWAY

THE harbour is crowded with ships.

Freighters from the Mediterranean, laden with cork and oil, cross the wake of blue- and gold-flagged ferries from Sweden, out-distance barges piled with wood from the forests of Finland. The Union Jack streams from a private yacht, the Stars and Stripes flies from a visiting training ship. Sunshine sparkles on the red flag of Russia, the Swastika of Germany, the white sails of a hundred pleasure craft. Out of all this bright congestion a steamer slowly draws out from the dock, and cautiously noses into the glittering traffic.

It is the steamer bearing us away.

The shore and not the vessel seems to move. The wharves and warehouses and bridges change their relation to each other. The Langelinie drifts by: its flowering shrubs blaze into tiny fires and disappear like puffs of smoke. Kaleidoscopic specks on the terrace in front of the Yacht Club pattern themselves into people and diminish into specks again. A sunbeam dances for a second on the little bronze mermaid seated on her rock, and then she, too, vanishes.

The spires of Hamlet's Castle begin to define themselves from the clouds floating beyond them. Many Danes, returning after sojourn in distant countries, straining their eyes for this first landmark of home, recognize it through tears. Many visitors, leaving Denmark, and watching this last landmark melt into the clouds, also find tears in their eyes.

Now all the spires of Copenhagen grow misty: no longer copper-green and gold but grey-blue, like the stuff that dreams are made on. Even as they dissolve—the dome of the Marble Church, the crown of the Christiansborg Palace, the flat-topped tower of the Cathedral, the pointed one of the Raad-hus, the twisted spiral of Our Saviour's—each still holds the dear familiar shape.

And so they will hold them always for those who love this kindest of kingdoms: her children, her adopted children, merchants, sailors, visitors who arrive in the morning and depart in the afternoon.

The towers of Copenhagen and the friendly shores of Denmark etherealize as time and distance intervene. But the blue outlines against a sky of paler blue do not wholly fade. The coast line does not lose its gentle curves. Like the tints painted upon porcelain and preserved beneath a glaze impervious to time, although invisible, so, protected by our affection, soft colours gleam upon smooth shapes.

"There is a delicious land."

Appendix

BRIEF CHRONOLOGICAL OUTLINE
OF DANISH HISTORY

PART I—PREHISTORIC

FOREST PERIOD

The interior was unpenetrated and the people lived along the edge of the water.

STONE AGE

Data obtained from kitchen middens, dolmens, and barrows.

BRONZE AGE

Forests penetrated, interior of Jutland opened. Islands of Fünen and Zealand opened. Soil cultivated. Arms and jewels found in barrows or tumuli. Also bodies of dead in roughly baked containers.

IRON AGE

Ships built. Horse introduced. Runes, derived from Phœnician alphabet, came into existence.

ROMAN INFLUENCE

Ornaments in gold and silver brought in and copied.

300 B.C.

Pytheas, a merchant from Massila (Marseilles), mentions Denmark, calling it Thule.

HEROIC AGE

Recorded in Icelandic sagas of eleventh and twelfth centuries. Also by Saxo, Danish chronicler of thirteenth century.

VIKINGS

Usual mingling of fact with legend. Many petty States, ruled over by Kings or Chiefs. Free men and serfs. Free men had National Gatherings or *Things* to settle public affairs.

Until eighth century tradition only. French and Anglo-Saxon chroniclers first to give authentic account of Denmark and Danes. Furnish records of Viking raids in France and England in time of Charlemagne.

PART II—MIDDLE AGES

826.

Christianity introduced by Ansgar, a Frankish monk, who had baptized Harald Klak, King of Jutland. Became Bishop of Hamburg and later of Bremen. Died in 865.

900.

Petty kingdoms welded together. (Jutland, islands, and what is now Southern Sweden.) Danevirke Wall built by Queen Thyra Danebod.

960.

Harald Bluetooth became King of Denmark. First Danish King to accept Christianity.

994.

Sweyn (Svend) Forkbeard laid siege to London unsuccessfully. Spent winter in Southampton. Bought off by heavy gold payment.

1002.

Sweyn returned to England.

1013.

Sweyn became master of England.

1015.

Canute the Great succeeded him. Left England—returned—reconquered it. Had ideal of Anglo-Scandinavian Empire with England at head.

1018.

Canute, at death of his brother Harald, succeeded to throne of Denmark.

1028.

Invaded Norway and annexed it. Canute died. Period of Civil War. Also attacks by savage tribes from south shores of Baltic.

1128.

Birth of Absalon.

1157.

King Valdemar the Great, mightiest potentate in Europe, with his son Canute VI, extended Denmark's borders to include Mecklenburg and Pomerania.

1176.

Founding of Copenhagen.

1202.

Valdemar the Conqueror included Estonia.

1320.

The Holsteinish Counts held mortgages sufficient to make them rulers of Denmark.

1340.

Niels Ebbesen killed Count Holstein.

1375.

Death of Valdemar Atterdag.

1380.

Margaret, daughter of King Valdemar, on the death of her husband Hakon VI, ruled over Norway. This union lasted four hundred years.

1387.

On the death of her son Oluf, Margaret reigned as Queen over Denmark.

1389.

Won war with Sweden and became sovereign of three Scandinavian countries.

1413.

Margaret died. Succeeded by her nephew, Erik of Pomerania, whom she had appointed.

1410–1435.

In retaliation of the toll levied by Erik on all vessels passing through the Sound, the Hanseatic League assisted the Holsteiners in their twenty-five years' war with Denmark.

1460–1864.

The Duchy of Holstein ruled by the House of Oldenburg, some of whose members were also Kings of Denmark.

1521–1523.

Sweden broke the union.

1533.

Death of Frederik I. The Kingdom without a King. Christian II was imprisoned. Lübeck and Copenhagen joined to liberate him. Lübeck played false and put two Germans (in succession) in Copenhagen.

1536.

Copenhagen besieged by Christian III. Surrendered to him. Roman Catholicism banished. The Reformation was accomplished.

1563–1570.

Wars with Sweden.

PART III—MODERN HISTORY

1645.

Denmark ceded Sweden one of her Swedish provinces, Halland, for 30 years, and Gotland, by Treaty of Brömsebro.

1652.

Charles X of Sweden (after a war with Poland) invaded Holstein. Spectacular surprise march across ice of Little Belt. Captured Odense, marched across the Store Belt, and occupied Copenhagen.

1658.

Truce arranged and treaty signed. Dissatisfied with treaty, Charles again attacked Denmark.

1660.

War ended with Treaty of Copenhagen. By it Denmark lost Scania, Halland, and several places on island of Rügen. Also forced to give Swedish ships free passage through the Sound.

1660–1661.

Bloodless reorganization of the Constitution upon principle of unrestricted monarchy. Similar to model of Louis XIV of France. More definitely outlined than in most other countries. War with Sweden. Danes invaded Scania, but forced to evacuate after the Battle of Lund.

1679.

Peace made, with position of combatants practically unchanged. Great loss of life and money.

1699.

Frederik IV invaded Holstein, which was ally of Sweden, but the Swedish King, Charles XII, attacked Zealand and forced peace.

1709.

Danes again invaded Holstein and Scania. Driven out of Scania by the peasants.

1711.

Great Plague. 23,000 dead.

1720.

Definite Treaty of Peace with Sweden signed at Stockholm.

1728.

Great Fire. More than one-quarter of houses in Copenhagen destroyed.

1780.

Pact of Armed Neutrality, headed by Catherine of Russia, by which Northern Nations, including Denmark, furnished naval supplies to France and Spain, with whom Great Britain was at war.

1782.

General Peace ended this dangerous situation.

1790–1800.

Radical reforms, advantageous to peasantry. Denmark a pioneer in this respect. Abolished African slave trade. First country to do this.

1795.

Second Great Fire.

1797.

A more liberal tariff. The first in the world to break away from mercantilism.

1801.

Lord Nelson fought Danish Fleet because of Denmark's part in armed neutrality of Northern Nations. Great Britain victorious.

1807.

England demands surrender of Danish Fleet, because of Denmark's sympathy with France and Russia. Copenhagen capitulated to British bombardment.

1807–1814.

Denmark allied herself with France for seven years' war against England. Danish trade paralysed as hostilities took place at sea.

1814.

Treaty of Peace at Kiel. Denmark ceded Norway to Sweden. Heligoland to England.

1814.

Congress of Vienna. Denmark gave Prussia Pomerania and Rügen for money and Duchy of Lauenburg. England restored to Denmark her possessions in East and West Indies.

1830.

Movement toward new Constitutional ideas.

1848.

Death of Christian VIII. Succeeded by Frederik VII.

1848.

Revolutionary uprisings in Europe.

1848.

Outbreak in Holstein against Denmark.

1848.

Duchies were supported by Germany, and Denmark was supported by Russia and other Scandinavian countries.

1848.

Armistice at Malmö. Duchies to be entrusted to a Commission: two Prussian, two Danish, and one elected by common consent.

1849.

Armistice denounced. Slesvig-Holsteiners oppressed Danish peasants. War between duchies, supported by Prussian troops and German confederation.

1849.

Another armistice.

1849.

Without bloodshed Denmark acquired a modern free Constitution (June 5).

1850.

Continual fighting between Danes and duchies.

1850.

Separate peace signed with Prussia. Integrity of Denmark guaranteed by England, France, Prussia, and Sweden.

1850.

Fighting continued. Battle of Isted. Danes victorious.

1850.

Tillisch tried to solve language difficulty.

1852.

Treaty signed in London, with representatives from England, France, Austria, Prussia, and Sweden to decide on succession for Danish throne in default of male heir.

1855.

Constitution amended.

1863.

Death of Frederik VII and accession of Christian IX.

1863.

Constitution amended.

1863.

Duke of Augustenburg assumed title of Frederik VIII (called Pretender). Backed by Slesvig and all of Germany, which repudiated London Treaty of 1852.

1863–1864.

Continual warfare. Prussian and Austrian forces against Denmark. Wrangel headed former and de Meza the Danish. Battle of Dybböl.

1864.

Peace Conference in London. No agreement reached and war resumed.

1864.

Denmark sued for peace. Signed at Vienna. Renounced all claims to Lauenburg, Holstein, and Slesvig (with Als) as far as Kongeaa. Waited for plebiscite in North Slesvig.

1866.

Constitution altered, in favour of wealthy class. Led to political struggle, which affected subsequent social and economic developments (favourably).

1866.

Austria, defeated by Prussia, ceded to Prussia all her real or supposed rights in Holstein by Treaty of Prague. Napoleon III intervened with reservation for plebiscite in Slesvig.

1878.

Prussia agreed with Austria to abrogate the treaty. Germany forbade Danish population of Slesvig to use Danish language, songs, or colours. Bought Danish land (in Slesvig) and settled Germans on it.

1898–1900.

Von Köller, Governor of Slesvig-Holstein, particularly arbitrary.

1901.

Parliamentary principle established as foundation of constitutional life.

1915.

Enfranchisement of women.

1919.

North Slesvig restored to Denmark after plebiscite with new frontiers by Treaty of Versailles.

1920.

King Christian of Denmark formally took possession of territory regained.

SALIENT FACTS AND STATISTICS

Area

The Kingdom of Denmark comprises an area of about 16,570 square miles. This is about one-third the size of England or about the size of Massachusetts and New Jersey combined. It is divided into two natural parts—the Peninsula of Jutland which is attached to the Continent of Europe, and the islands which lie between Jutland and Scandinavia. Copenhagen is situated on the largest of them, Zealand. In all, there are some five hundred islands in the Kingdom, including the Faroe Islands in the Atlantic and Bornholm in the Baltic, but only about one hundred are inhabited. Iceland is a sovereign state in union with Denmark. The King of Denmark is also King of Iceland.

Geographical Position and Temperature

Denmark lies between latitudes 54 ° 33' and 57° 45' North and between longitudes 8° 4' 54" and 12° 47' 25" East. The climate is mild and moist with an average year-round temperature of 45° F. —in many ways similar to that of South Scotland. The average rainfall is about 24 inches.

Form of Government

Denmark is a constitutional monarchy. Executive power is vested in the King through his twelve Ministers. Legislative authority rests jointly with the Crown and the Rigsdag, the latter consisting of the Folketing, or House of Representatives, with 149 members, and the Landsting, or Senate, with 76 members. All Danish subjects over twenty-five years of age have the franchise to the Folketing but must be over thirty-five before they can vote in the Landsting elections. The proportional system is used for all elections. No Government is possible in Denmark if not upheld by a majority in the Folketing. At present, four main parties are represented in Parliament—the Conservatives, the Liberal Lefts, the Radical Lefts, and the Social Democrats. Denmark has been ruled since 1929 by a Social Democrat-Radical Coalition, and the Social Democrats were returned to power in the general election of October 1935 with an increased majority.

Population

The total population of Denmark in 1935 was 3,705,559. Of this number 779,512 live in Copenhagen, 867,389 in the provincial towns, and 2,058,658 in the rural areas.

Occupation

Agriculture and fishing support about 1,200,000 of the inhabitants of Denmark and approximately 1,100,000 are engaged in industry and the handicrafts.

Religion

The Evangelical Lutheran is the established Church of Denmark and is supported by the State Roman Catholics. Reformist Jews and Methodists are recognized by the Government and have the right to solemnize marriages which are valid according to Danish law.

Topographical Division

Denmark is a country without mountains and with no large rivers. The highest elevation (Himmelbjerget) is 500 feet, and the largest river is the Gudenaa, less than 80 miles in length.

Division of Land

Of the country's whole area about 80 per cent is occupied by farms and 10 per cent by forests.

Currency and Weights and Measures

The currency is the Danish Krone which is divided into Öre at the rate of 100 Öre to the Krone. Denmark adheres to the Sterling Group and the Krone is slightly depreciated in terms of the pound sterling. Since 1910 the metric system of weights and measures has been in official use.

BIBLIOGRAPHY

HISTORY AND POLITICS

Bain, Robert N.: *Scandinavia: A Political History of Denmark, Norway and Sweden from 1900.* Cambridge University Press, London, 1905.

Brown, John: *The Northern Courts.* Constable & Co., Ltd., London, 1818.

Dulles, Allen W. and Armstrong, H. F.: *Can We Be Neutral?* (American Council on Foreign Relations.) Harper & Brothers, New York, 1936.

Egan, Maurice F.: *Ten Years near the Frontier.* George H. Doran Company, New York, 1919.

Hill, Mary: *Margaret of Denmark, 1397–1412.* T. Fisher Unwin, London, 1898.

Larson, Laurence Marcellus: *Canute the Great, 995–1035, and the Rise of Danish Imperialism during the Viking Age.* G. P. Putnam's Sons, New York, 1912.

Nors, P.: *The Court of Christian VII of Denmark,* edited by E. Steen. Hurst & Blackett, Ltd., London, 1928.

Otté, Elise C.: *Denmark and Iceland.* Rivingtons, London, 1881.

Otté, Elise C.: *Norway, Sweden and Denmark,* edited by E. S. Corwin; Polar Research by G. T. Surface. P. F. Collier & Son, New York, 1916.

Riis, Jacob August: *Hero Tales of the Far North.* The Macmillan Company, New York, 1915.

Saxo Grammaticus: *The Nine Books of the Danish History of Saxo Grammaticus,* translated by Oliver Elton. Norroena Society, London and New York, 1905.

Stefansson, Jón: *Denmark and Sweden, with Iceland and Finland.* G. P. Putnam's Sons, New York, 1917.

Weitemeyer, Harald: *Denmark; Its History.* William Heinemann, Ltd., London, 1891.

GUIDE AND TRAVEL BOOKS

Baedeker, Karl: *Norway, Sweden and Denmark*. Charles Scribner's Sons, New York, 1912.

Brochner, Georg: *Wayfarer in Denmark*. Methuen & Company, Ltd., London, 1932.

Denmark, 1934. Royal Danish Ministry for Foreign Affairs and the Danish Statistical Department, Copenhagen, 1934.

Desmond, Shaw: *The Soul of Denmark*. Charles Scribner's Sons, New York, 1918.

Edelberg, Max, ed.: *Denmark in Word and Picture*, translated by W. E. Calvert. C. A. Reitzels Forlag, Copenhagen, 1935.

Gosse, Edmund W.: *Two Visits to Denmark*. Smith, Elder & Co., London, 1917.

Harvey, William J. and Reppian, Christian: *Denmark and the Danes*. T. Fisher Unwin, London, 1915.

Riis, Jacob August: *The Old Town*. The Macmillan Company, New York, 1909.

Williams, Ethel Carleton: *Denmark and the Danes*. Methuen & Company, Ltd., London, 1932.

ECONOMICS INCLUDING
CO-OPERATION AND SOCIAL INSURANCE

Falk, I. S.: *Security against Sickness*. Doubleday, Doran & Company, Inc., New York, 1936.

Howe, Frederic C.: *Denmark: The Co-operative Way*. Coward-McCann, Inc., New York, 1936.

LITERATURE

Bay, Jens Christian: *Denmark in English and American Literature: A Bibliography*. Danish-American Association, Chicago, 1915.

Bergstrom, Hjalmar: *Karen Bornemann; Lyngaard & Co.*, two plays translated from the Danish. Mitchell Kennerley, New York, 1913.

Brandes, Georg: *Creative Spirits of the Nineteenth Century*. The Thomas Y. Crowell Company, New York, 1923.

Brandes, Georg: *Eminent Authors of the Nineteenth Century*, translated by R. B. Anderson. The Thomas Y. Crowell Company, New York, 1886.

A Book of Danish Verse, from Oehlenschläger to Johannes V. Jensen, translated by S. Foster Damon and Robert Silliman Hillyer, selected

Bibliography 259

and annotated by Oluf Friis. The American-Scandinavian Foundation, New York, 1922.

Comedies by Holberg: Jeppe of the Hill; The Political Tinker; Erasmus Montanus, translated by Oscar James Campbell, Jr. and Frederic Schenck. The American-Scandinavian Foundation, New York, 1914.

Danish Ballads, translated by E. M. Smith-Dampier, Cambridge University Press, London, 1920.

Drachmann, Holger: *Renaissance* (a melodrama), translated by Lee M. Hollander. *Poet-Lore,* vol. XIX, no. IV, pp. 369–419, Boston, 1908.

Gosse, Edmund W.: *Studies in the Literature of Northern Europe.* C. Kegan Paul & Co., London, 1879.

Hertz, Henrik: *King René's Daughter* (a Danish lyrical drama). Walter H. Baker Company, Boston, 1892.

Holberg, Baron Ludvig: *Three Comedies,* translated by H. W. L. Hime. Longmans, Green & Company, London and New York, 1912.

Hustvedt, Sigurd Bernhard: *Ballad Criticism in Scandinavia and Great Britain during the Eighteenth Century.* The American-Scandinavian Foundation, New York, 1916.

Kierkegaard, Sören: *Philosophical Fragments,* translated by David F. Swenson. Princeton University Press, Princeton, 1936.

Larsen, Hanna Astrup: *Scandinavian Literature.* American Library Association, Chicago, 1930.

Les Vieux Chants Populaires Scandinaves. Oxford University Press, London, 1896.

Oehlenschläger, Adam: *Axel and Valborg* (an historical tragedy), translated by F. S. Kolle. Grafton Press, New York, 1906.

Oehlenschläger, Adam: *Correggio* (a tragedy), translated by Theodore Martin. Parker & Son, Oxford, 1854.

Oehlenschläger, Adam: *The Gods of the North* (an epic poem), translated by W. E. Frye. Pickering & Inglis, London, 1845.

Olrik, Axel: *The Heroic Legends of Denmark,* translated by Lee M. Hollander. Oxford University Press, London, 1919.

Sigurjónssón, Jóhan: *Modern Icelandic Plays: Eyvind of the Hills* and *The Hraun Farm,* translated by Henninge Krohn Schanche. The American-Scandinavian Foundation, New York, 1916.

Sturluson, Snorri: *The Prose Edda,* translated from the Old Icelandic by Arthur Gilchrist Brodeur. The American-Scandinavian Foundation, New York, 1929.

Topsoe-Jensen, H. G.: *Scandinavian Literature I.* Scandinavian Classics, George Allen & Unwin, Ltd., London, 1930.

Topsoe-Jensen, H. G.: *Scandinavian Literature from Brandes to Our Day.* George Allen & Unwin, Ltd., London; The American-Scandinavian Foundation, New York, 1929.

Werrenrath, Reinald, ed.: *One Hundred Modern Scandinavian Songs.* Oliver Ditson Co., Inc., New York, 1925

Wied, Gustav: 2 × 2 = 5 (a comedy), translated by Ernest Boyd and Holger Kopell. Nicholas L. Brown, New York, 1923.

THE ARTS

Danish Folk Dances. School of Civics and Philanthropy, Chicago, 1917.

Hammerich, Angul: *Mediæval Musical Relics of Denmark,* translated by Margaret Williams Hamerik. Breitkopf & Härtel, Leipzig, 1912.

Hayden, Arthur: *Chats on Royal Copenhagen Porcelain.* T. Fisher Unwin, London, 1918.

Hayden, Arthur: *Royal Copenhagen Porcelain, Its History and Development from the 18th Century.* T. Fisher Unwin, London, 1911.

Mantzius, Karl: *A History of Theatrical Art in Ancient and Modern Times,* translated by L. von Gossel. Gerald Duckworth & Co., Ltd., London, 1903.

Modern Danish Architecture, edited by Kay Fisker and F. R. Yerbury. Ernest Benn, Ltd., London, 1927.

Scandinavian Art: A Survey of Swedish Art, by Carl G. Laurin; *Danish Art in the Nineteenth Century,* by Emil Hannover; *Modern Norwegian Art,* by Jens Thiis. The American-Scandinavian Foundation, New York, 1922.

JUVENILES

Andersen, Hans Christian: *Fairy Tales.* J. M. Dent & Sons, Ltd., London, 1906.

Andersen, Hans Christian: *Fairy Tales and Other Stories,* revised and in part newly translated by W. A. and J. K. Craigie. Oxford University Press, London, 1914.

Andersen, Hans Christian: *Fairy Tales and Other Stories,* translated by H. L. Braekstad. Century Company, New York, 1900.

Andersen, Hans Christian: *Fairy Tales and Stories,* edited by Signe Toksvig. The Macmillan Company, New York, 1921.

Danish Fairy and Folk Tales, compiled by Jens Christian Bay from the Danish of Svend Grundtvig, E. T. Kristensen, etc. Harper & Brothers, New York, 1899.

East of the Sun and West of the Moon. The Macmillan Company, New York, 1928.

Grundtvig, Svend: *Danish Fairy Tales,* translated by J. G. Cramer. Four Seas Company, Boston, 1919.

Michaëlis, Karin: *Bibi.* Doubleday, Doran & Company, Inc., New York, 1927.

Owen, Ruth Bryan (Kammerjunkerinde Rohde): *Denmark Caravan.* Dodd, Mead & Company, Inc., New York, 1936.

FICTION

Works of Hans Christian Andersen. Houghton Mifflin Company, Boston, 1884.

Bergsöe, Vilhelm: *The Bride of Roervig,* translated by N. Francis. Guildford, London, 1877.

Bergsöe, Vilhelm: *Pillone,* translated by D. G. Hubbard. Lovell, New York, 1883.

Dinesen, Isak: *Seven Gothic Tales.* Harrison Smith & Robert Haas, Inc., New York, 1934.

Drachmann, Holger: *Nanna, A Story of Danish Love.* A. C. McClurg & Company, Chicago, 1901.

Drachmann, Holger: *The Cruise of the Wild Duck.* T. Fisher Unwin, London, 1893.

Ewald, Carl: *My Little Boy,* translated by Alexander Teixeira de Mattos. Charles Scribner's Sons, New York, 1912.

Ewald, Carl: *The Four Seasons,* translated by Alexander Teixeira de Mattos. Dodd, Mead & Company, Inc., New York, 1913.

Ewald, Carl: *The Old Room,* translated by Alexander Teixeira de Mattos. Charles Scribner's Sons, New York, 1908.

Ewald, Carl: *The Old Willow Tree,* translated by Alexander Teixeira de Mattos. Thornton Butterworth, Ltd., London, 1929.

Ewald, Carl: *The Pond and Other Stories,* translated by Alexander Teixeira de Mattos. Thornton Butterworth, Ltd., London, 1929.

Ewald, Carl: *The Queen Bee and Other Nature Stories,* translated by G. C. Moore Smith. Thomas Nelson & Sons, London, 1908.

Ewald, Carl: *The Spider and Other Tales,* translated by Alexander Teixeira de Mattos. Charles Scribner's Sons, New York, 1907.

Ewald, Carl: *Twelve Sisters and Other Stories,* translated by Alexander Teixeira de Mattos. Thornton Butterworth, Ltd., London, 1929.

Ewald, Carl: *Two Legs,* translated by Alexander Teixeira de Mattos. Thornton Butterworth, Ltd., London, 1930.

Gjellerup, Karl Adolph: *Minna,* translated by C. L. Nielsen. William Heinemann, Ltd., London, 1913.

Gjellerup, Karl Adolph: *The Pilgrim Kaminita* (a legendary romance), translated by J. E. Logie; E. P. Dutton & Co., Inc., New York, 1912.

Gudmundsson, Kristmann: *Morning of Life,* translated by Elizabeth Sprigge and Claude Napier. Doubleday, Doran & Company, Inc., New York, 1936.

Gunnarsson, Gunnar: *Guest the One-Eyed,* translated by W. W. Worster. Alfred A. Knopf, Inc., New York, 1922.

Gunnarsson, Gunnar: *Seven Days' Darkness,* translated by Roberts Tapley. The Macmillan Company, New York, 1931.

Gunnarsson, Gunnar: *The Sworn Brothers,* translated by C. Field and W. Emmé. Alfred A. Knopf, Inc., New York, 1921.

Jacobsen, Jens Peter: *Marie Grubbe, A Lady of the Seventeenth Century,* translated by Hanna Astrup Larsen. Alfred A. Knopf, Inc., New York, 1925.

Jacobsen, Jens Peter: *Mogens and Other Stories,* translated by Anna Grabow. Nicholas L. Brown, New York, 1921.

Jacobsen, Jens Peter: *Niels Lyhne,* translated by Hanna Astrup Larsen. The American-Scandinavian Foundation, New York, 1919.

Jensen, Johannes V.: *Fall of the King,* translated by P. T. Federspiel and Patrick Kirwan. Henry Holt & Company, Inc., New York, 1933.

Jensen, Johannes V.: *The Long Journey:* Vol I, *Fire and Ice;* Vol. II, *The Cimbrians;* Vol. III, *Christopher Columbus,* translated by A. G. Chater. Alfred A. Knopf, Inc., New York, 1923–1924.

Larsen, Hanna Astrup, ed.: *Denmark's Best Stories.* The American-Scandinavian Foundation, New York, 1928.

Larsen, J. Anker: *The Philosopher's Stone,* translated by A. G. Chater. Alfred A. Knopf, Inc., New York, 1924.

Lauesen, Marcus: *The Very Beautiful Days,* translated by Ingrid Modin. Cassell & Co., Ltd., London, 1934.

Loti, Pierre: *Iceland Fisherman.* A. L. Burt Company, Inc., New York, 1899.

Neumann, Robert: *The Queen's Doctor,* translated by Edwin and Willa Muir. Victor Gollancz, Ltd., London, 1936; Alfred A. Knopf, Inc., New York, 1937.

Nexö, Martin Andersen: *Ditte: Daughter of Man,* translated by A. G. Chater and Richard Thirsk. Henry Holt & Company, Inc., New York, 1921.

Nexö, Martin Andersen: *Ditte: Girl Alive!* Henry Holt & Company, Inc., New York, 1920.

Nexö: Martin Andersen: *Ditte: Towards the Stars,* translated by Asta and Rowland Kenney. Henry Holt & Company, Inc., New York, 1922.

Nexö, Martin Andersen: *In God's Land,* translated by Thomas Seltzer. Peter Smith, New York, 1933.

Nexö, Martin Andersen: *Pelle the Conqueror,* translated by Jesse Muir and Bernard Miall. Peter Smith, New York, 1930.

Pontoppidan, Henrik: *Apothecary's Daughters,* translated by Gordius Trelsen. Trübner & Co., London, 1889.

Pontoppidan, Henrik: *Emanuel; or, Children of the Soil,* translated by Mrs. Edgar Lucas. J. M. Dent & Sons, Ltd., London, 1892.

Pontoppidan, Henrik: *The Promised Land,* translated by Mrs. Edgar Lucas. J. M. Dent & Sons, Ltd., London, 1896.

Soiberg, Harry: *Sea King,* translated by Edwin Bjorkman. William Morrow & Co., Inc., New York, 1928.

Stuckenberg, Viggo Henrik Fog: *By the Wayside,* translated by Una Hook. Chatto & Windus, London, 1917.

BIOGRAPHY

Ady, Julia Cartwright (Mrs. Henry Ady): *Christina of Denmark* (Duchess of Milan and Lorraine). E. P. Dutton & Co., Inc., New York, 1913.

Andersen, Hans Christian: *Story of My Life.* Houghton Mifflin Company, Boston, 1871.

Andersen, Hans Christian: *The True Story of My Life,* translated by Mary Howitt. The American-Scandinavian Foundation, New York, 1926.

Autobiography of Johannes Jorgensen, translated by Ingeborg Lund. Sheed & Ward, New York, 1932.

Bain, Robert Nisbet: *Hans Christian Andersen.* Dodd, Mead & Company, Inc., New York, 1895.

Brandes, Georg: *Reminiscences of My Childhood and Youth,* translated by G. M. Fox-Davies. Duffield & Co., New York, 1906.

Gade, John A.: *Christian IV, King of Denmark and Norway.* George Allen & Unwin, Ltd., London; Riverside Press, Cambridge, 1920.

Moritzen, Julius: *Georg Brandes in Life and Letters.* Colyer, Newark, 1922.

Sandemose, Aksel: *A Fugitive Crosses His Tracks,* translated by Eugene Gay-Tifft. Alfred A. Knopf, Inc., New York, 1936.

Toksvig, Signe: *Life of Hans Christian Andersen.* Harcourt, Brace & Company, New York, 1934.

Wilkins, William Henry: *A Queen of Tears, Caroline Matilda.* Longmans, Green & Company, London and New York, 1904.

Wraxall, Sir Frederick C. L.: *Life and Times of Her Majesty Caroline Matilda.* W. H. Allen & Co., London, 1864.

GREENLAND AND
COLONIAL POSSESSIONS

Berlin, Knud: *Denmark's Right to Greenland.* Oxford University Press, London, 1932.

Birket-Smith, Kaj: *The Eskimos.* E. P. Dutton & Co., Inc., New York, 1936.

Freuchen, Peter: *Arctic Adventure.* Farrar & Rinehart, Inc., New York, 1935.

Freuchen, Peter: *Eskimo,* translated by A. Paul Maerker-Branden. Horace Liveright, Inc., New York, 1931.

Friis, Achton and Larsen, Johannes: *De Danskes Oer.* Gyldendal, Copenhagen, 1927.

Georgi, Johannes: *Mid-Ice,* translated by F. H. Lyon. E. P. Dutton & Co., Inc., New York, 1936.

Gjerset, Knut: *History of Iceland.* George Allen & Unwin, Ltd., London, 1922.

Greenland. Editors: M. Vahl, G. C. Andrup, L. Bosé, Ad. S. Jensen. Published by the Commission for the Direction of the Geological and Geographical Investigation of Iceland; Humphrey Milford, London; Oxford University Press, 1928.

Hutchison, Isobel W.: *On Greenland's Closed Shore.* William Blackwood & Sons, Ltd., London, 1930.

Jenness, Dr. Diamond: *People of the Twilight.* The Macmillan Company, New York, 1928.

Kent, Rockwell: *Greenland.* Harcourt, Brace & Company, Inc., New York, 1932.

Kent, Rockwell: *N by E.* Harcourt, Brace & Company, Inc., New York, 1930.

Kent, Rockwell: *Salamina.* Harcourt, Brace & Company, Inc., New York, 1935.

Lindsay, Martin: *Those Greenland Days.* William Blackwood & Sons, Ltd., London, 1932.

Nansen, Fridtjof: *First Crossing of Greenland.* Longmans, Green & Company, London, 1890.

Owen, Ruth Bryan: *Leaves from a Greenland Diary.* Dodd, Mead & Company, Inc., New York, 1935.

Rasmussen, Knud Johan Victor: *Across Arctic America.* G. P. Putnam's Sons, New York, 1927.

Stefansson, Vilhjalmur: *My Life with the Eskimos.* The Macmillan Company, New York, 1913.

Tansill, C. C.: *Purchase of the Danish West Indies.* Johns Hopkins Press, Baltimore, 1932.

AGRICULTURE

Branson, Eugene C.: *Farm Life Abroad: Field Letters from Germany, Denmark and France.* University of North Carolina Press, Chapel Hill, 1924.

Denmark Agriculture. The Agricultural Council, Copenhagen, 1935.

Foght, Harold Waldstein: *Rural Denmark and Its Schools.* The Macmillan Company, New York, 1915.

Haggard, Sir Henry Rider: *Rural Denmark and Its Lessons.* Longmans, Green & Company, New York, 1913.

EDUCATION

Begtrup, Holger; Lund, Hans; and Manniche, Peter: *The Folk High Schools of Denmark and the Development of a Farming Community.* Oxford University Press, London, 1929.

Campbell, Mrs. Olive D.: *The Danish Folk School.* The Macmillan Company, New York, 1928.

Education in Denmark, edited by Andreas Boje, Ernst J. Borup, Holger Rutzebeck. Oxford University Press, London, 1932.

Hart, Joseph K.: *Light from the North.* Henry Holt & Company, New York, 1926.

Hegland, Martin: *Danish People's High School.* Government Printing Office, Washington, 1915.

Howe, Frederic C.: *Denmark: A Co-operative Commonwealth.* Harcourt, Brace & Company, New York, 1921.

Knight, Edgar W.: *Among the Danes.* University of North Carolina Press, Chapel Hill, 1927.

INDEX

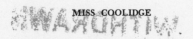

(Some of these titles have been published under the names of either
Agnes Edwards *or* Agnes Edwards Rothery.)